Gandhi *in* Raza

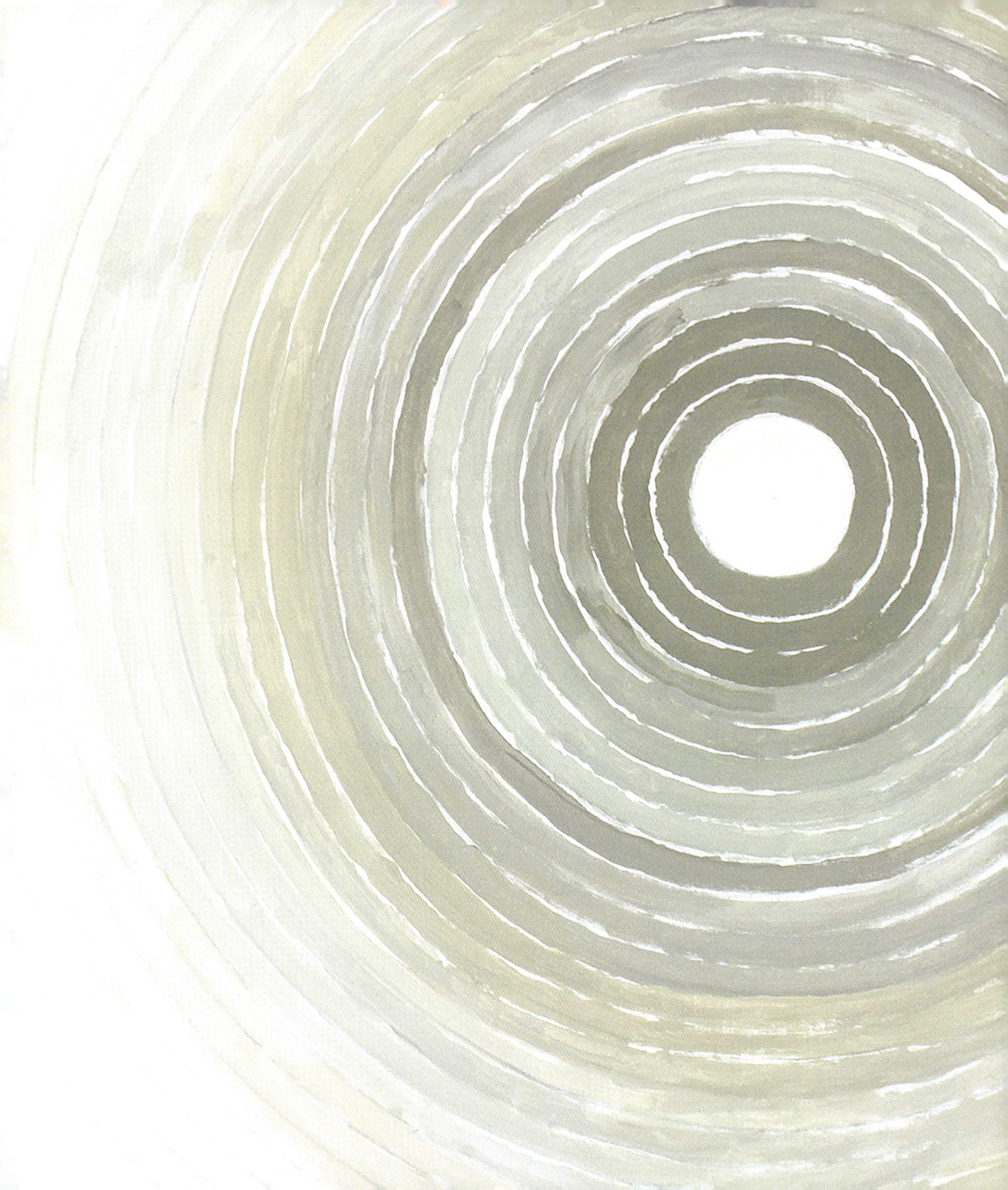

Gandhi in Raza

Nandalal Bose • Gopalkrishna Gandhi
Ashok Vajpeyi • SH Raza

ākār prakār
Mapin
रज़ा फाउण्डेशन | The Raza Foundation

First published in 2017 by
Akar Prakar

in collaboration with
Raza Foundation

in association with
Mapin Publishing

in conjunction with a show titled "Gandhi in Raza"
at the India Habitat Centre, New Delhi on the occasion of the 95th birth anniversary of S H Raza. The show will be on display at Akar Prakar Art Advisory from 1st - 31st March, 2017.

Simultaneously published in the United States of America in 2017 by
Grantha Corporation
E: mapin@mapinpub.com

Distributed in North America by
Antique Collectors' Club
T: + 1 800 252 5231 | E: sales@antiquecc.com
www.accdistribution.com/us

Distributed in United Kingdom and Europe by
Gazelle Book Services Ltd.
T: +44 1524 68765 | E: sales@gazellebooks.co.uk
www.gazellebookservices.co.uk

Distributed in Thailand, Laos, Cambodia, Myanmar by
Paragon Asia Co. Ltd
T: +66 2 877 7755 | E: info@paragonasia.com

Distributed in Malaysia by
Areca Books
T: +60 4 2610307 | E: arecabooks@gmail.com
www.arecabooks.com

Distributed in the Rest of the World by
Mapin Publishing Pvt. Ltd
706, Kaivanna
Panchvati, Ellisbridge
Ahmedabad-380006
T: +91 79 4022 8228 | F: +91 79 4022 8201
E: mapin@mapinpub.com
www.mapinpub.com

ISBN: 978-93-85360-32-9 (Mapin)
ISBN: 978-1-935677-90-1 (Grantha)
LCCN: 2017934151

Copyediting: Ashok Vajpeyi
Proofreading: Ankona Das
Editorial support: Akar Prakar and Raza Foundation
Archival research: Raza Foundation
Book design: Bena Sareen
Printed at Archana, New Delhi

Captions:
Front Cover: S H Raza, 'Shanti', 2013
Frontispiece: S H Raza, 'Satyamev Jayte', 2012
Back Cover: S H Raza, 'Satya', 2012

Akar Prakar
P 238 Hindustan Park
Kolkata-700029
Gallery timing: 2-7 pm (Sunday closed)
T: +91 33 2464 2617
E: info@akarprakar.com
www.akarprakar.com

Akar Prakar Art Advisory
29 Hauz Khaz Village, 1st Floor
New Delhi -110016
Gallery timing: 11am-7 pm (Sunday closed)
T: +91 11 2686 8558
E: akarprakarartadvisory@gmail.com

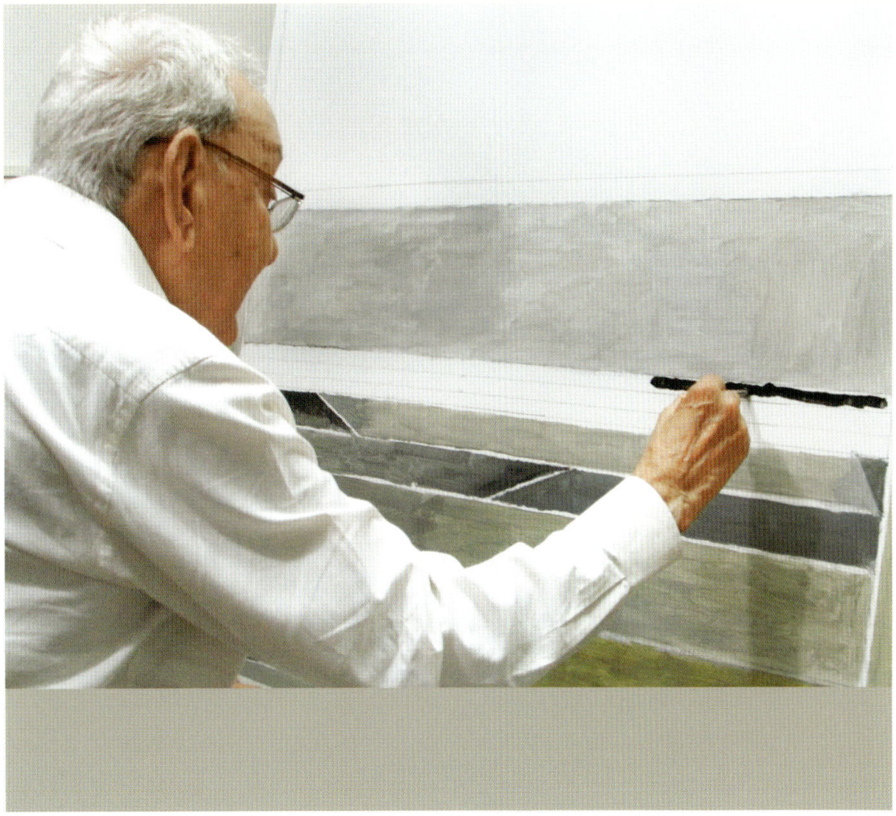

Contents

...mais entends

ce qui soufflé,

le message ininterrompu

Qui se forge de silence.

...But listen

to the voice of the wind,

and the ceaseless message

That forms itself out of silence.

~Rainer Maria Rilke

(Duino Elegies, The First Elegy)

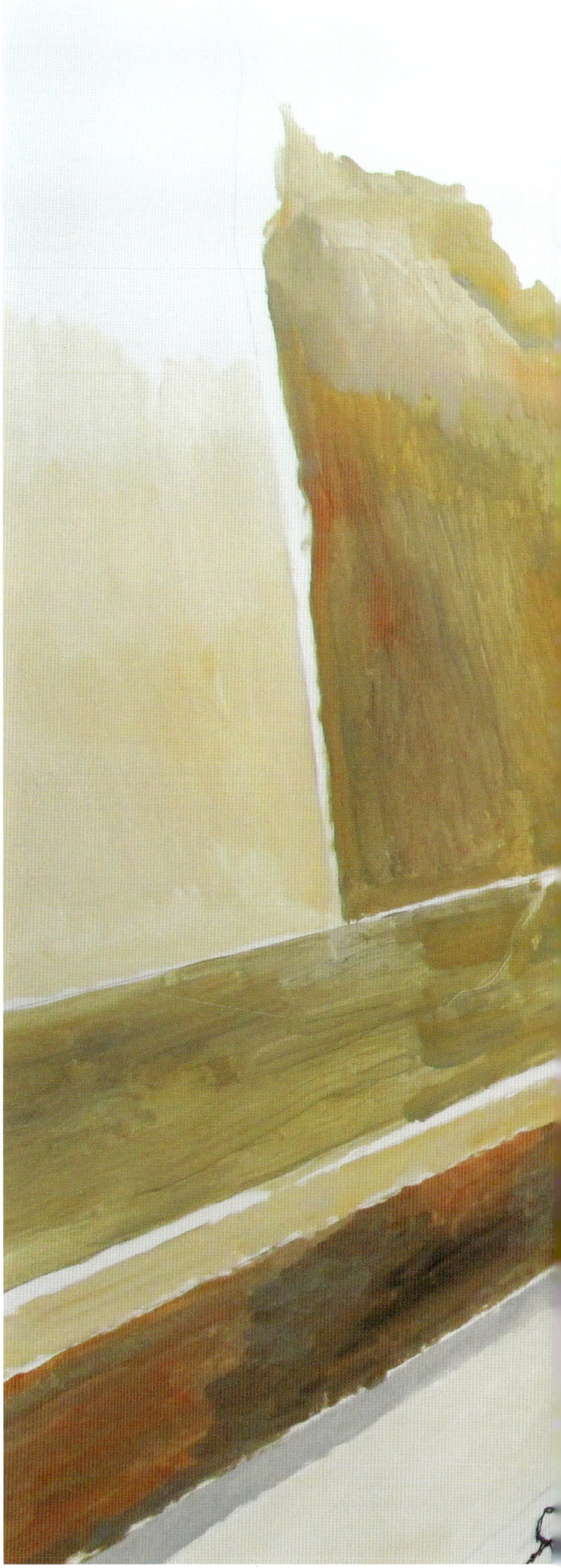

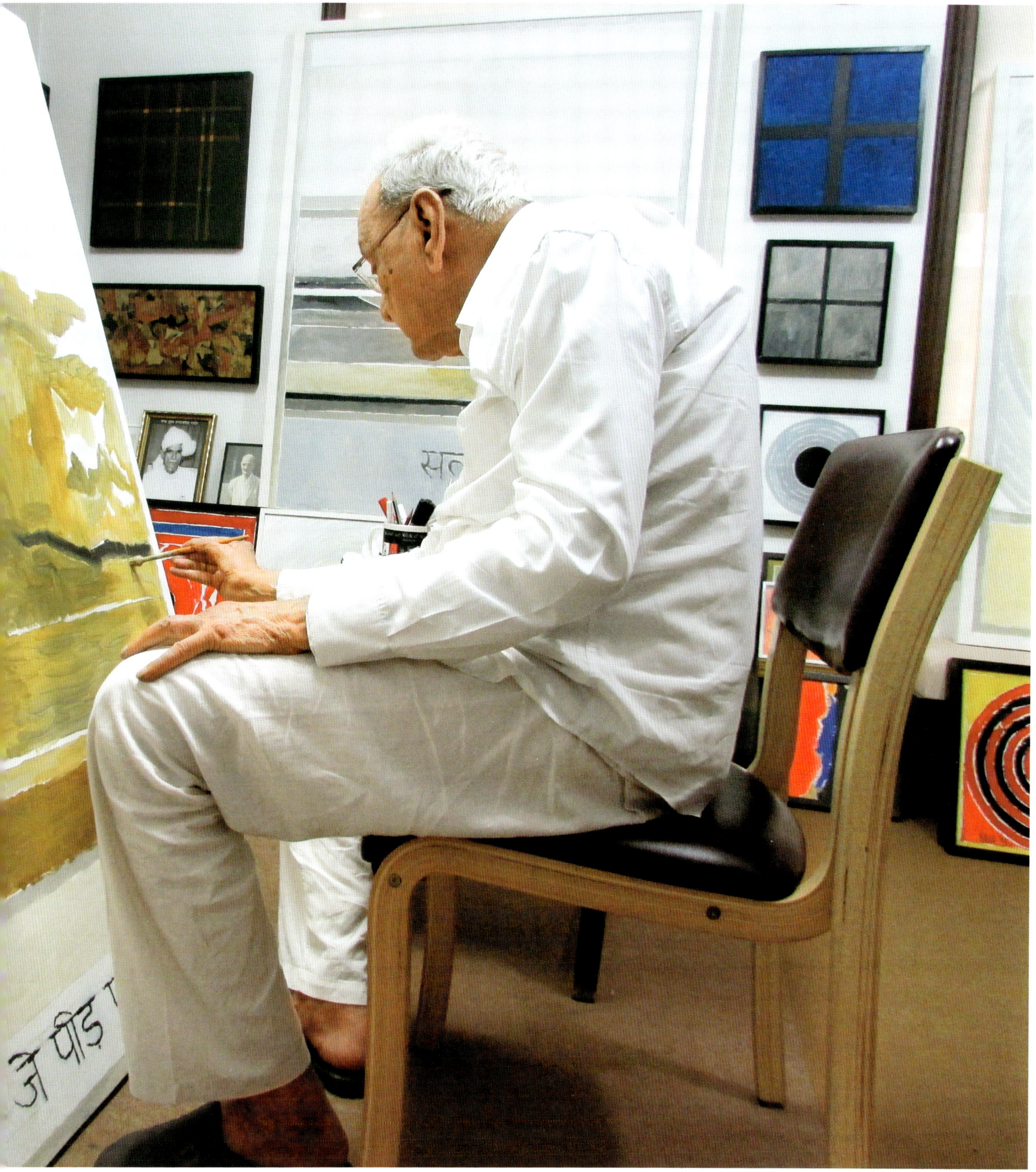

One late afternoon in 2013, barely two years after his residence in India, I found him doing a canvas in very subdued hues. I was intrigued since his usual geometrical shapes were not there...The painting in question was the first one which had the last words of the Mahatma as he fell down dead to the bullets of his assassin saying "Hey Ram". It is appropriately somber, subtly refuses to be an end-of-it-all work: it has a significant use of white—indicating both purity and hope but also engulfing the canvas with the mist or cloud of sadness. The solid column seems to suggest a certain defiance and stubbornness: the body killed but the spirit surviving.

—Ashok Vajpeyi

'HEY RAM' ACRYLIC ON CANVAS 23.5 x 23.5" 2013

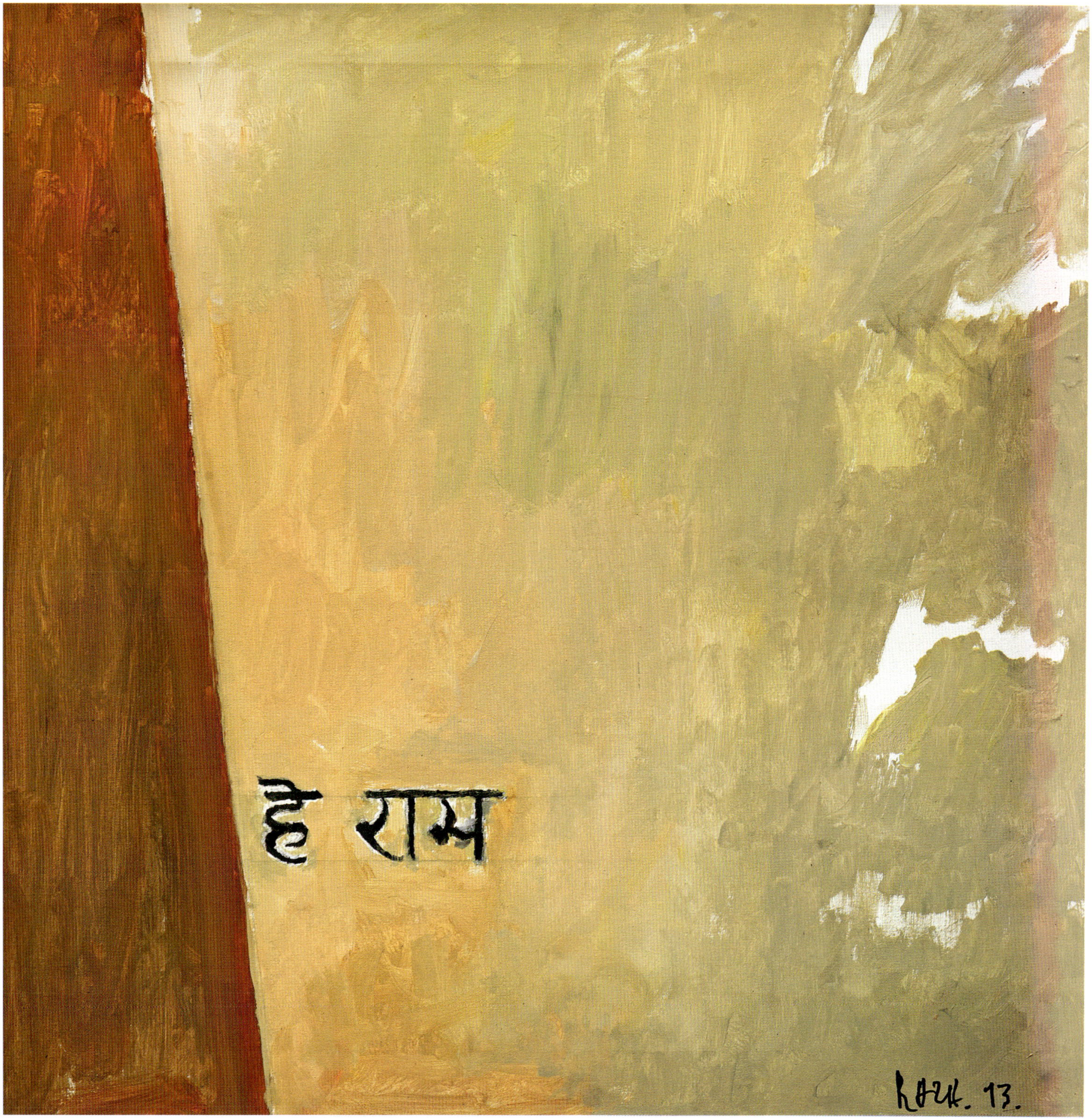
हे राम

...Raza's work is totally abstract; its many layers perhaps indicating that truth can be reached or felt only after passing and struggling through many layers of effort and darkness visualized in thick layers coming across even when one knows that it is near.

—Ashok Vajpeyi

'SATYA' ACRYLIC ON CANVAS 59 x 47.25" 2013

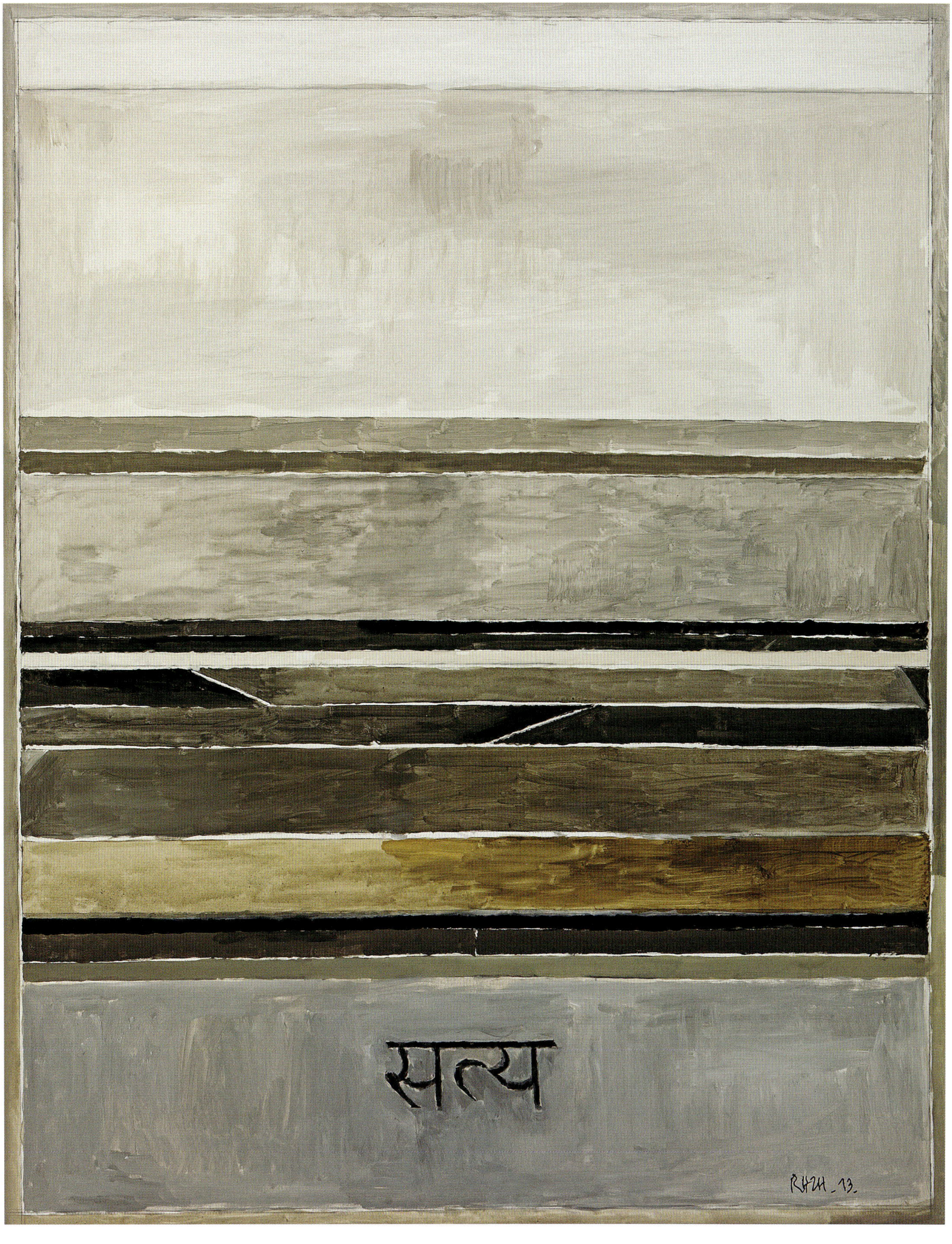
सत्य
RAZA_13.

In 'Shanti' Raza recapitulates his old theme of peace—the heart of being as he perceives it. He strongly believed that energy, centralized as it was for him in *bindu*, flows from and towards peace.

—Ashok Vajpeyi

'SHANTI' ACRYLIC ON CANVAS 59 x 47.25" 2013

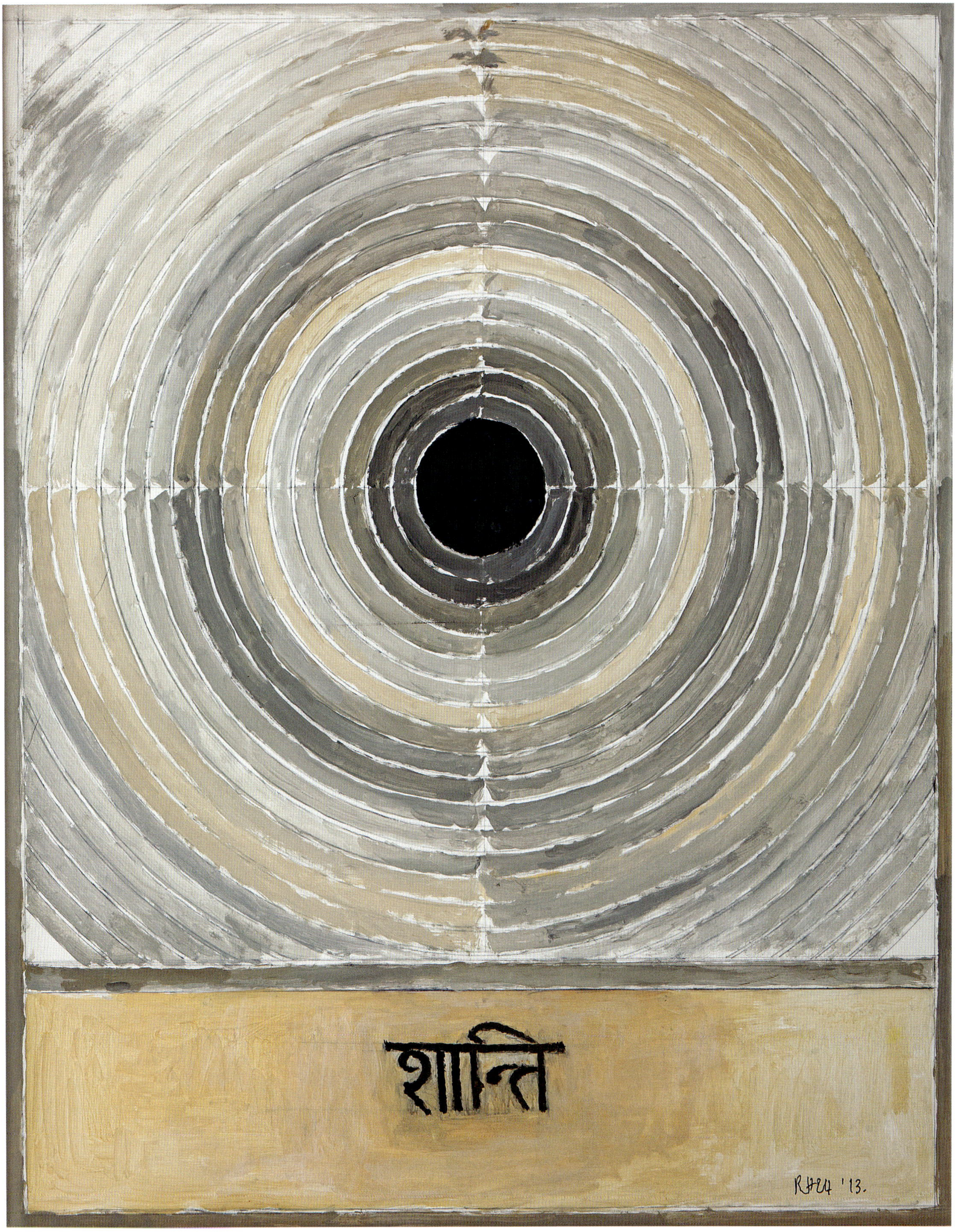
शान्ति

...inspired by the famous Narsi Mehta verse, a favourite of the Mahatma,
defining the true men of God as those who understood the pain of others.
...It is remarkable that there is no didactic intention but only an invocation,
also subtly communicating the difficulty of feeling the pain
of the other, 'Peed Parai'.

—Ashok Vajpeyi

'PEED PARAI' ACRYLIC ON CANVAS 59 x 59" 2013

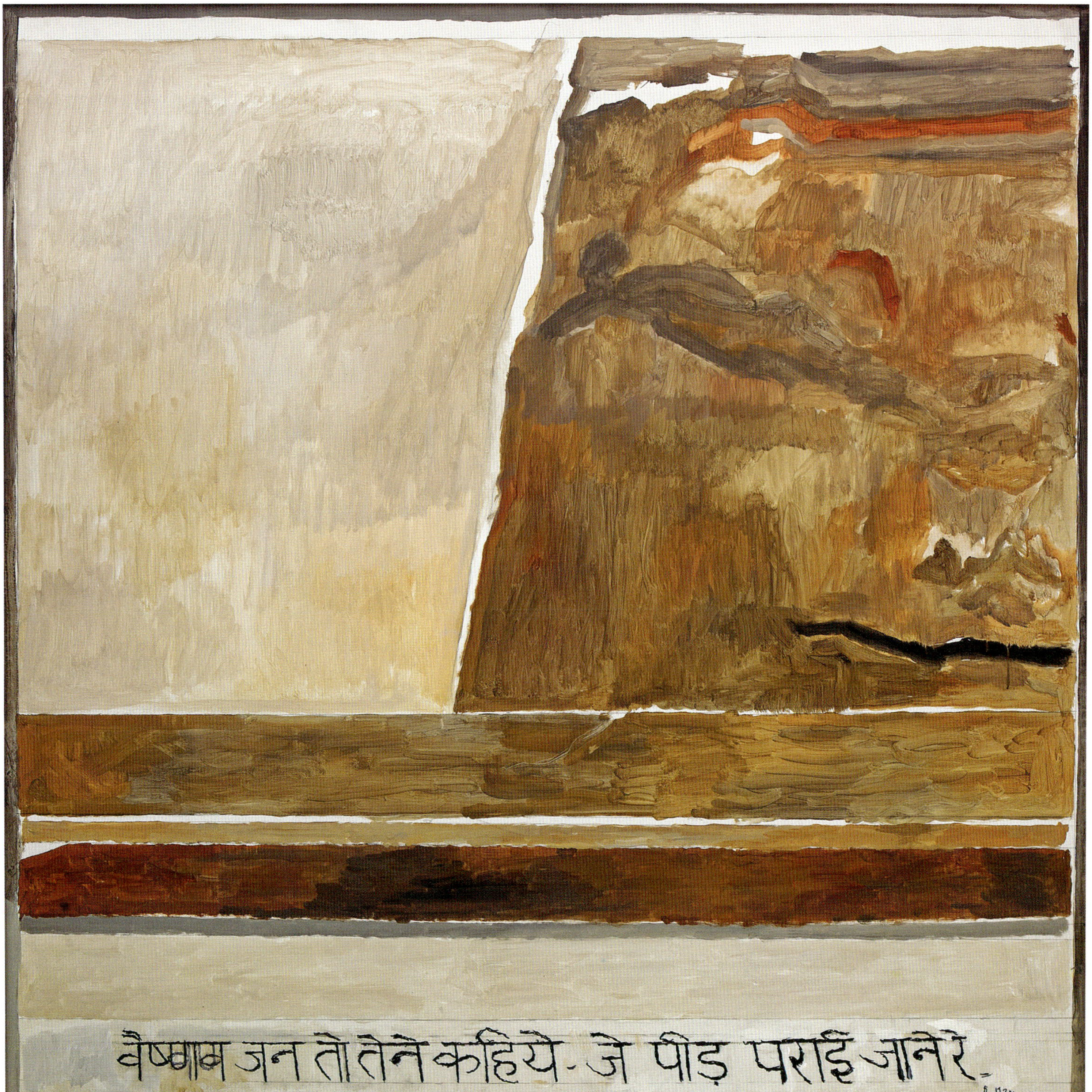
वैष्णव जन तो तेने कहिये - जे पीड़ पराई जाने रे -

...Raza returns to his spiritual geometry by creating a vibrant image to embody a bold idea taken from a favourite *bhajan* of the Mahatma. Instead of eulogizing Ram, as the verse does, Raza picks up for visual manifestation the key concept of the *bhajan*:

Ishwar Allah Tero Nam,

Sabako Sanmati De Bhagawan.

—Ashok Vajpeyi

'SANMATI' ACRYLIC ON CANVAS 59 x 59" 2013

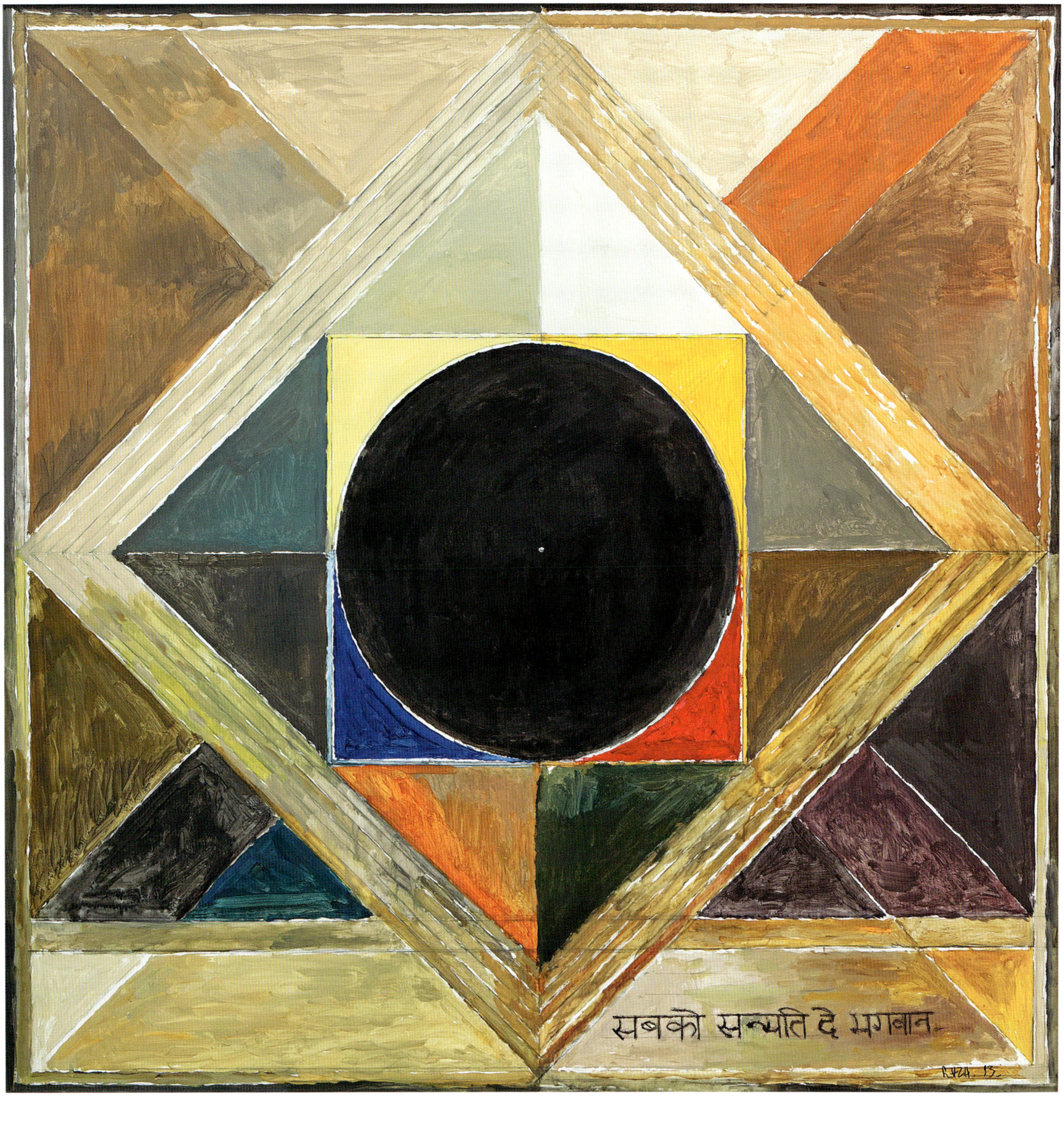
सबको सन्मति दे भगवान
RAZA. 13.

Swadharma was a favourite concept of Raza which he picked from Vinoba Bhave. He felt that everyone should sooner or later discover his/her *swadharma* and act accordingly. His own *dharma*, he was clear, was to paint and he stuck to it throughout his life.

—Ashok Vajpeyi

'SWADHARM' ACRYLIC ON CANVAS 59 x 59" 2013

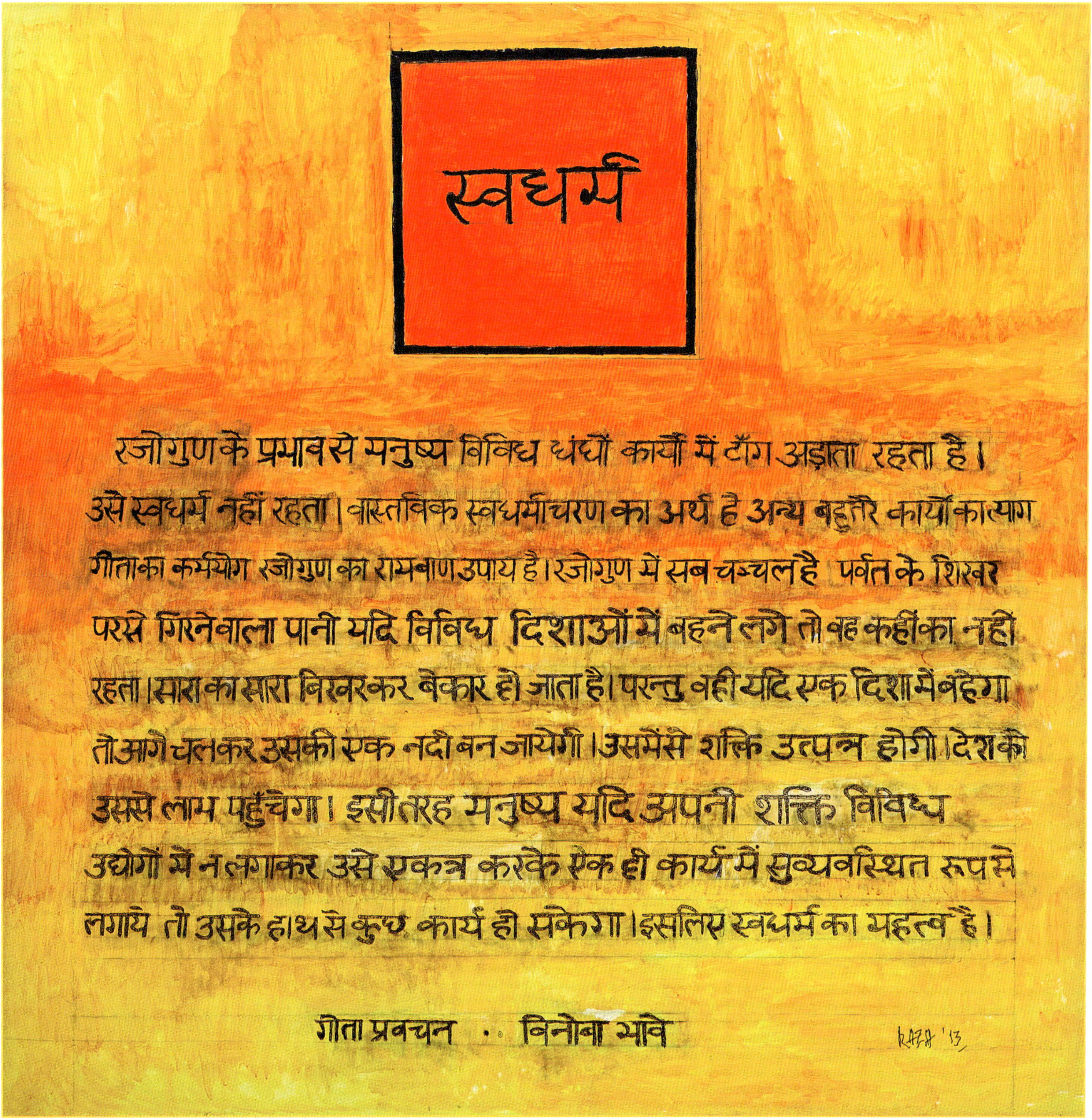
स्वधर्म
रजोगुण के प्रभाव से मनुष्य विविध धंधों कार्यों में टाँग अड़ाता रहता है।
उसे स्वधर्म नहीं रहता। वास्तविक स्वधर्माचरण का अर्थ है अन्य बहुतेरे कार्यों का त्याग
गीता का कर्मयोग रजोगुण का रामबाण उपाय है। रजोगुण में सब चञ्चल है पर्वत के शिखर
परसे गिरनेवाला पानी यदि विविध दिशाओं में बहने लगे तो वह कहीं का नहीं
रहता। सारा का सारा बिखरकर बेकार हो जाता है। परन्तु वही यदि एक दिशा में बहेगा
तो आगे चलकर उसकी एक नदी बन जायेगी। उसमेंसे शक्ति उत्पन्न होगी। देश को
उससे लाभ पहुँचेगा। इसी तरह मनुष्य यदि अपनी शक्ति विविध
उद्योगों में न लगाकर उसे एकत्र करके एक ही कार्य में सुव्यवस्थित रूप से
लगाये, तो उसके हाथ से कुछ कार्य हो सकेगा। इसलिए स्वधर्म का महत्व है।
गीता प्रवचन · विनोबा भावे
RAZA '13

As a painter Raza felt fascinated by words
and always treated them with awe and regard. The words of the
Mahatma were for him almost holy scripture and he put them on the
canvas on a painted background but in full primacy.

—Ashok Vajpeyi

'THOUGHTS OF GANDHI JI' ACRYLIC ON CANVAS 59 x 47.25" 2013

सत्य हर इन्सान के हृदय में निवास करता है। उसे वहीं खोजना चाहिये और सत्य जैसा किसी को नज़र आता वैसे ही उससे संचालित होना चाहिये। पर किसी को अधिकार नहीं है कि वह दूसरों को मजबूर करे कि वे उसे जैसा सत्य दिखायी देता है उसके मुताबिक चलें।

सन्तोष कोशिश करने में, है पाने में नहीं। पूरी कोशिश पूरी जीत होती है।

मैं रास्ता जानता हूँ। वह सीधा और सँकरा है। वह तलवार की धार सरीखा है। मुझे उसपर चलने में मज़ा आता है। जब फिसलता हूँ तो रोता हूँ।

क्यों आसान है नीचे गिरना या नीचे फिसलना
ऊपर उठने से, सीढ़ी दर सीढ़ी ?

वही बचेगा जो मैंने किया, वह नहीं जो मैंने कहा या लिखा।

जहाँ प्यार है, वहीं ईश्वर है।

महात्मा गांधी.

Raza '13,

A group of seven paintings is a kind of *parikrama*
(circumambulation) by a painter around a great soul,
a Mahatma who always inspired him;
a noble venture around an ennobling theme.

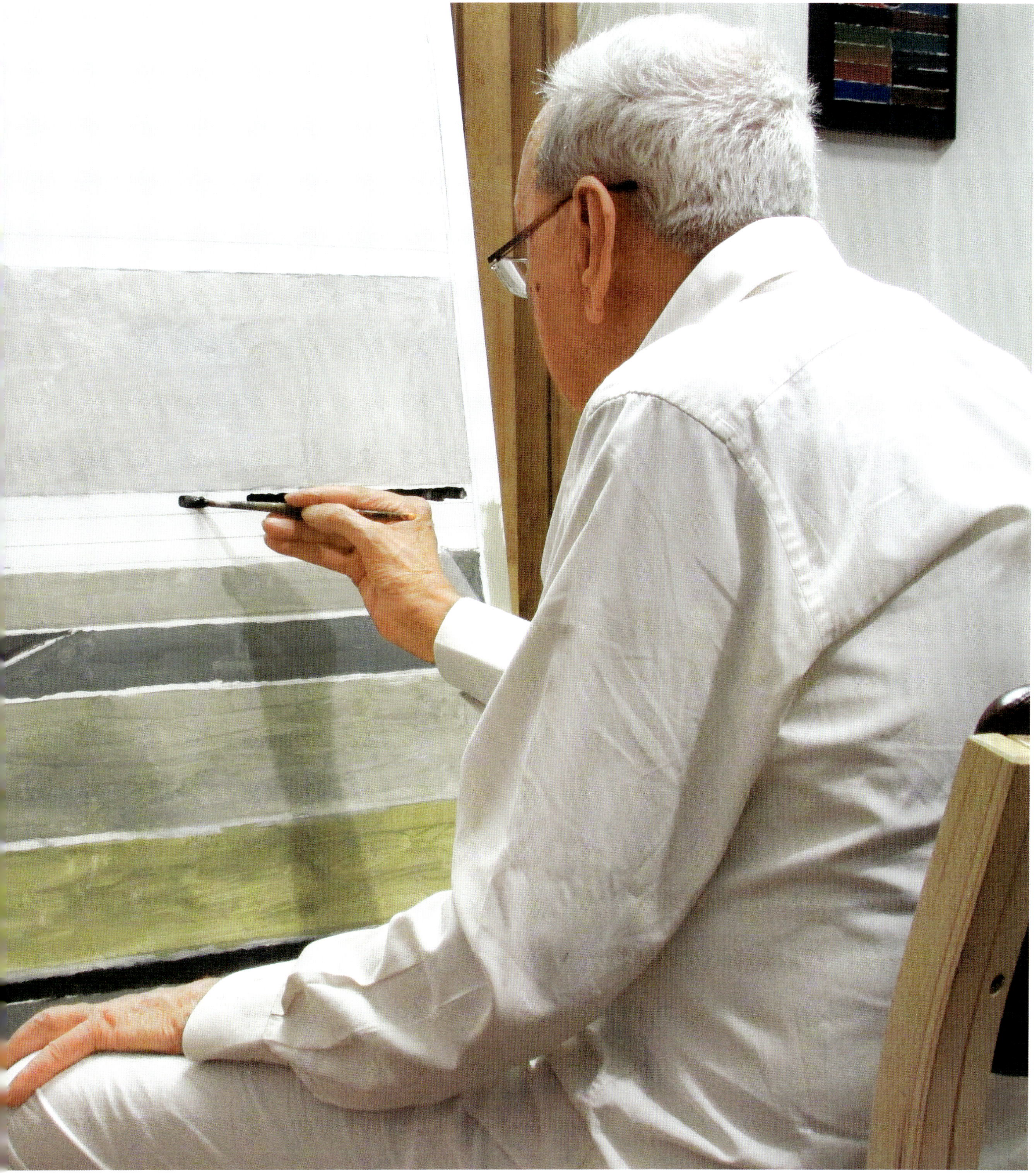

Life, Art and Gandhian Light ASHOK VAJPEYI

The iconic Indian modern painter Sayed Haider Raza saw Mahatma Gandhi in Mandla, Madhya Pradesh when he was barely 8 years old. The Mahatma had come there to address a public meeting during the freedom struggle of India. Raza's father was a forest official of the British Government. The young Raza accompanied by a forest official to the meeting was accosted by the wife of a British official of the Forest Department who had rightly guessed that the boy was going to the meeting of the Mahatma. Raza later could not recall what he heard in the public speech of the Mahatma but the image of the Mahatma with his *laathi* and half-naked *faquir* body remained deeply etched in his mind.

India attained freedom on 15th August, 1947 but was also, most unfortunately, partitioned. Huge migrations took place as also did communal tensions and riots. Raza's brothers, a sister and his first wife, all living in India had their houses attacked and vandalized. They all decided to move to Pakistan. Raza, however, refused to shift to Pakistan staying as he said, in his own country, in his "Watan". Once when I probed deeper into the reason why he did not leave India with his family members, Raza confessed reluctantly that he thought he would be betraying the Mahatma if he left the nation! The image of the Mahatma remained stuck in Raza's mind even after about 17 years when he first saw him. It reminds me of what the eminent historian Irfan Habib said in a lecture entitled 'Gandhi's Finest Hour' in 2015: "It appeared as if, between danger and peace, only one man was standing and obviously it was Gandhiji. And, therefore, for us and specially for Muslims (and I am one of them) Gandhiji was the person who was responsible for us remaining in India and alive."

Raza always believed that partition of India was a great mistake and the assassination of the Mahatma by a Hindu zealot, a great tragedy. In an interview when Raza was turning 80 years of age, I asked him of his greatest disappointments, to which he said:

> *My greatest disappointments, akin to un-happiness, were in 1948 when Mahatma Gandhi was assassinated. It was an act of an individual who had convictions of his own. It came at a time when we were full of youth and energy. We wanted to take our destinies in hand and in the period of immense enthusiasm and joy, this tragic event took place. I don't know of any of other distress, more important, in my life. We had a sense of void and despair, a sense of sheer outrage. It was, I remember, the same years when I lost my parents. As children we were not politically conscious. And for different reasons coming from the authority of my father we were really away from any social work or political action. But the national pride was there, the desire to be independent was there. Mahatma Gandhi had mobilized the country as one magnificent source of power. The British with all their might had to leave India and it was independent. And then the father of the nation was killed. No other incident had this acute pain and distress in my life.*

He used to visit Sewagram or Sabarmati or Rajghat whenever he came to India on his frequent sojourns to his native country from France, where he spent nearly six decades of his life. For him visiting a Gandhi place was like visiting a temple or a mosque or any holy place. Even when he was well above 85 years of age, some of us have watched him kneel down and touch the earth with his forehead in salutation to the Mahatma. He, of course, had read the Mahatma's auto-biography *My Experiments with Truth* and would delve through the Mahatma's treatise on the great metaphysical poem Geeta. His constant engagement with the spiritual and philosophical vision of Gandhiji also led him to discover and study the Mahatma's spiritual heir, Acharya Vinoba Bhave. He became particularly fond of the concept of *swadharma* propounded by Vinobaji. One of the few books he brought from Paris when he shifted to Delhi to spend his last five-and-a-half years was Vinobaji's book *Geeta Pravachan* in Hindi.

Raza was agonizingly aware of the declining impact of Gandhiji on contemporary Indian life, religion, politics and thought it was a great and tragic betrayal of the Mahatma. He firmly believed that the Mahatma was the tallest and greatest Indian born in the millennia. He often, both in Paris and India, used to interrogate me about this renouncing of Gandhiji by contemporary India.

In mid 1970s in Paris, when Raza was firmly acknowledged as a painter of Ecole d'Paris, he felt uncomfortable and agonized. He asked himself: Where was India in him? And where was Raza in his work? He turned to some Indian concepts notably to *bindu* which later became his iconic mark as a painter. Along with *bindu* came other concepts significantly, *shanti* being one of them, inspired him, every now and then, and also resulted in a large number of his paintings. There are reasons to believe that the concept of *shanti* was a Gandhian concept combining the Mahatma's other two favourite concepts of truth and violence into one.

Raza was a deeply religious man. The modernism, both in the West and India, was dominated by loss of faith marked by disruptions, dissonance and dislocation, tension and fury. Raza evolved an alternative modernism rooted in faith and peace, in consonance and celebration. This innate spirituality has a multi-religious address. Until the end of his life, almost every weak Raza used to visit a Church, a temple and a mosque sitting or standing in deep meditation. He firmly believed that creativity cannot manifest itself fully unless blessed by divine powers. Raza did not observe any rituals but sought through different religions true and enduring spiritual communion. Here again I feel that the unique spiritual institution the Mahatma created in the 'Prarthana Sabha' with renditions of multi-religious scriptures and meditative silence was the inspiration behind Raza's practice. Raza, more than once, mentioned to me that he fully agreed with the Gandhian thought that all religions were true but they were also all imperfect. This allowed space and opportunity to all the religions to learn from each other in humility and accommodation. Raza was not just a Muslim keeping intact his faith in Islam, but also a person inspired by and rooted in metaphysical concepts of Hinduism and, occasionally, Christianity.

Raza's unfailing and spontaneous generosity was already a legend in his life time. While jealously protecting the autonomy and privacy of his self, both in life and art, he ceaselessly cared for others. He went out of his way and means to assist others. It is in keeping with this life-long concern for others that he devoted a lot of his resources to the Raza Foundation and left all immovable and movable properties, after his death, to the Raza Foundation. Raza was not an austere person like the Mahatma. Raza enjoyed all the good things of life without failing to take care of others and respond warmly whenever called upon to help. Like once when a couple of years ago Lord Meghnad Desai started raising funds for a Mahatma Gandhi statue to be installed in Westminster, London, Raza readily contributed a sum of Rs. 10 lakhs. In essence this was again a Gandhian trait. We would recall that the Mahatma also was extremely generous in spirit and thought and

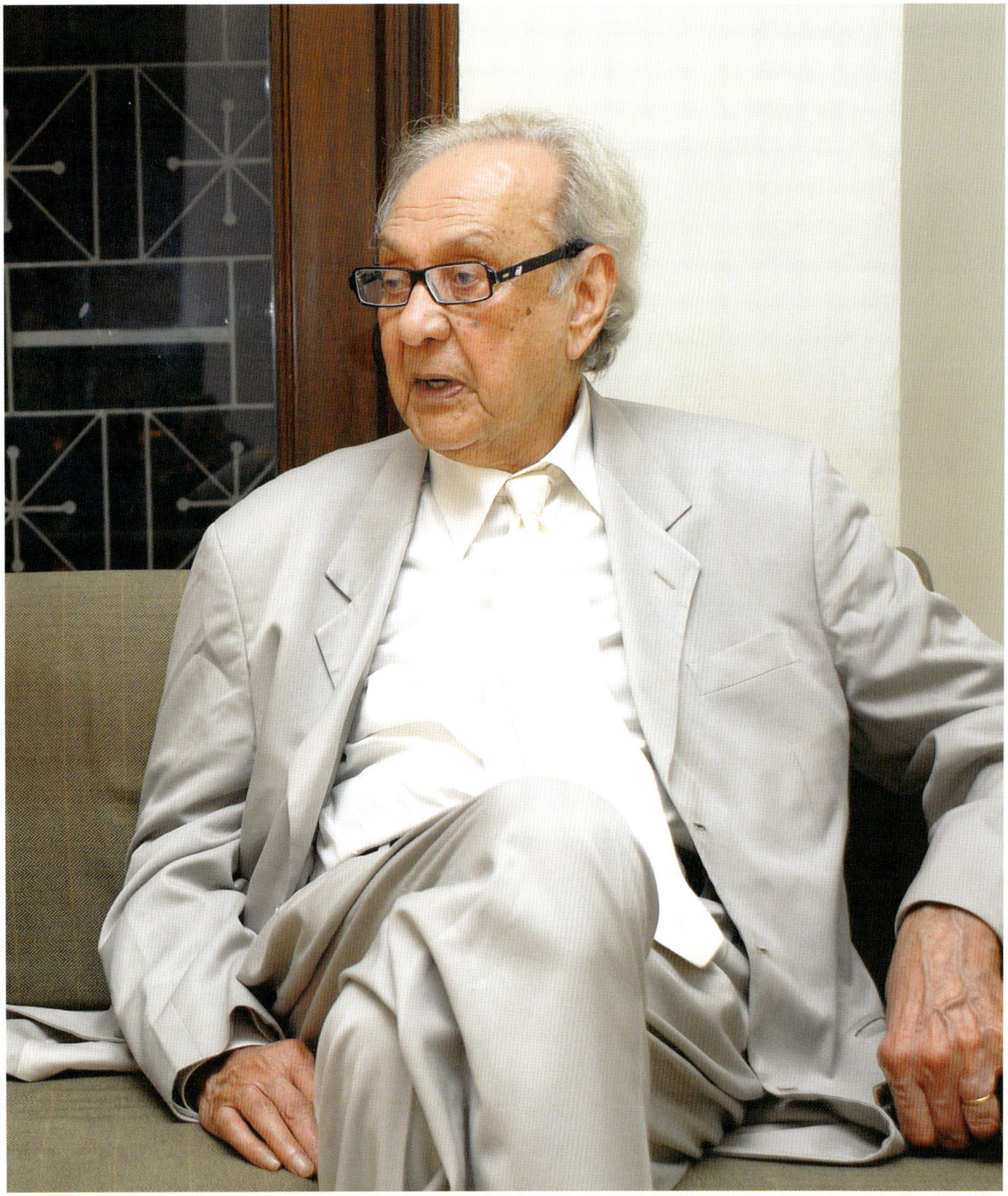

answered every single communication sent to him by all and sundry. Like the Mahatma, though through the poetry of Rainer Maria Rilke, Raza would insist on paying heed to the inner voice, sometimes lying buried in our soul. A poem of Rilke, as quoted below, to that effect used to be the daily prayer which Raza would recite before he started work in his studio.

> *....But listen*
> *to the whisperings of the wind,*
> *and the ceaseless message*
> *That forms itself out of silence.*
> —An extract from *The First Elegy* (originally *Duino Elegies*)

Raza decided to return to his homeland in 2011 and he spent the last five-and-a-half years of his life and art in Delhi. He settled down in a house he had bought earlier and registered it in the name of the Raza Foundation in Safdarjung Development Area near Haus Khas. I became almost a daily visitor, a friend who spent almost every evening with him when he would finish his work for the day. He would sit with his glass of wine and I with mine of whiskey. We chatted many times, spent a lot of time in silence and many a time discussing the work-in-progress or looking for a title for his recently finished painting. Sometimes I would read out to him verses of Kabir, Ghalib, Mir etc., also, once in a while a selection of thoughts of the Mahatma. Since he used to feel excited at Gandhian ideas with his face glowing with sudden illumination, I once suggested him to do a set of paintings on or inspired by the key ideas of the Mahatma. He nodded in agreement.

One late afternoon in 2013, barely two years after his residence in India, I found him doing a canvas in very subdued hues. I was intrigued since his usual geometrical shapes were not there. When we met in the evening he told me that he had decided to do a set of Gandhi paintings. The painting in question was the first one which had the last words of the Mahatma as he fell down dead to the bullets of his assassin saying "Hey Ram". It is appropriately somber, subtly refuses to be an end-of-it-all work: it has a significant use of white—indicating both purity and hope but also engulfing the canvas with the mist or cloud of sadness. The solid column seems to suggest a certain defiance and stubbornness: the body killed but the spirit surviving.

The next in the series was inspired by the famous Narsi Mehta verse, a favourite of the Mahatma, defining the true men of God as those who understood the pain of others. Raza himself had been a person who had always responded to the suffering or plight of others with ready help and empathy. So the verse not only resonated with the saint poet and the Mahatma, to whom the tribute was directed, but also with his own attitude. In a self-created convention of inscribing words or more often lines of verses on paper, Raza inscribes the first line of a poem on the canvas. It is remarkable that there is no didactic intention but only an invocation, also subtly communicating the difficulty of feeling the pain of the other, 'Peed Parai'.

In the third work in the series, Raza returns to his spiritual geometry by creating a vibrant image to embody a bold idea taken from a favourite *bhajan* of the Mahatma. Instead of eulogizing Ram, as the verse does, Raza picks up for visual manifestation the key concept of the *bhajan*:

Ishwar Allah Tero Nam,

Sabako Sanmati De Bhagawan.

The lines above, meaning—Ishwar and Allah are your names, may god grant wise knowledge to all—appropriately use the word *sanmati*, meaning wise knowledge, a knowledge contemporary India seems to have lost and yet it badly needs to possess, a visual and deeply Gandhian reminder that God is one, though named and articulated differently in different religions.

Before the painting entitled 'Satya' was painted we had some discussion on how truth is a very abstract idea, uniquely human and there are many versions of and approaches to it. There are many claimants: philosophy, morality, religion, spirituality, literature, arts, science etc. We noted that the Mahatma's relationship with truth had its own dynamics. Initially and for a long while he believed 'God is truth' but later, in a significantly transformative move, he espoused 'Truth is God'. Raza's work is totally abstract; its many layers perhaps indicating that truth can be reached or felt only after passing and struggling through many layers of effort and darkness visualized in thick layers coming across even when one knows that it is near. One also cannot possibly miss the purity and whiteness, when the light of truth is attained.

In the next work 'Shanti', Raza recapitulates his old theme of peace—the heart of being as he perceives it. He strongly believed that energy, centralized as it was for him in *bindu*, flows from and towards peace. *Swadharma* was a favourite concept of Raza which he picked from Vinoba Bhave. He felt that everyone should sooner or later discover his/her *swadharma* and act accordingly. His own *dharma*, he was clear,

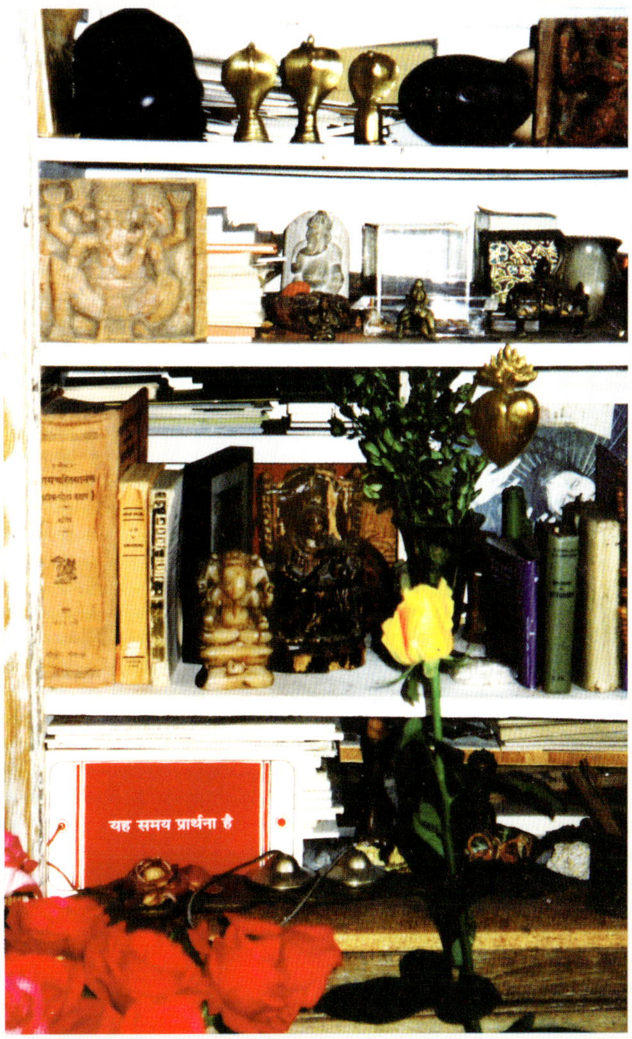
यह समय प्रार्थना है

was to paint and he stuck to it throughout his life. The painting carries an extract from Vinoba Bhave's *Geeta Pravachan*. The painting with its colours almost ablaze tends to suggest that you glow only after you have realized your *swadharma*. Raza puts just the words on the page. At 91 years of age he struggled hard to write all the words on the canvas.

Out of the many quotes from Gandhi's thoughts, Raza chose a few which he thought resonated even today. They were originally in English. After he chose some of them I translated them into Hindi. Like the Mahatma, Raza had a deep love for and abiding confidence in his mother tongue, Hindi. Barring very few exceptions, he always inscribed Hindi, Sanskrit and Urdu words or verses in Devnagri; hardly ever in Roman or English or French. As a painter Raza felt fascinated by words and always treated them with awe and regard. The words of the Mahatma were for him almost holy scripture and he put them on the canvas on a painted background but in full primacy.

Before these seven paintings Raza had only once painted on a Gandhian theme. In 1990 during his Indian visit he happened to meet the great philosopher Ramchandra Gandhi (a grandson of the Mahatma) at the bar in the India International Centre. Ramu, as we used to endearingly call him, gave him a new greeting card with an inscription of Gandhi in the following words:

In the midst of death life persists,
In the midst of untruth truth persists,
In the midst of darkness light persists.

Later in the same year Raza did, what may be called, his first Gandhian painting.

A group of seven paintings is a kind of *parikrama* (circumambulation) by a painter around a great soul, a Mahatma who always inspired him; a noble venture around an ennobling theme.

~

In the midst of death life persists,
In the midst of untruth truth persists,
In the midst of darkness light persists.

~Mahatma Gandhi

My greatest disappointments,
akin to un-happiness, were in 1948 when
Mahatma Gandhi was assassinated.
—Sayed Haider Raza

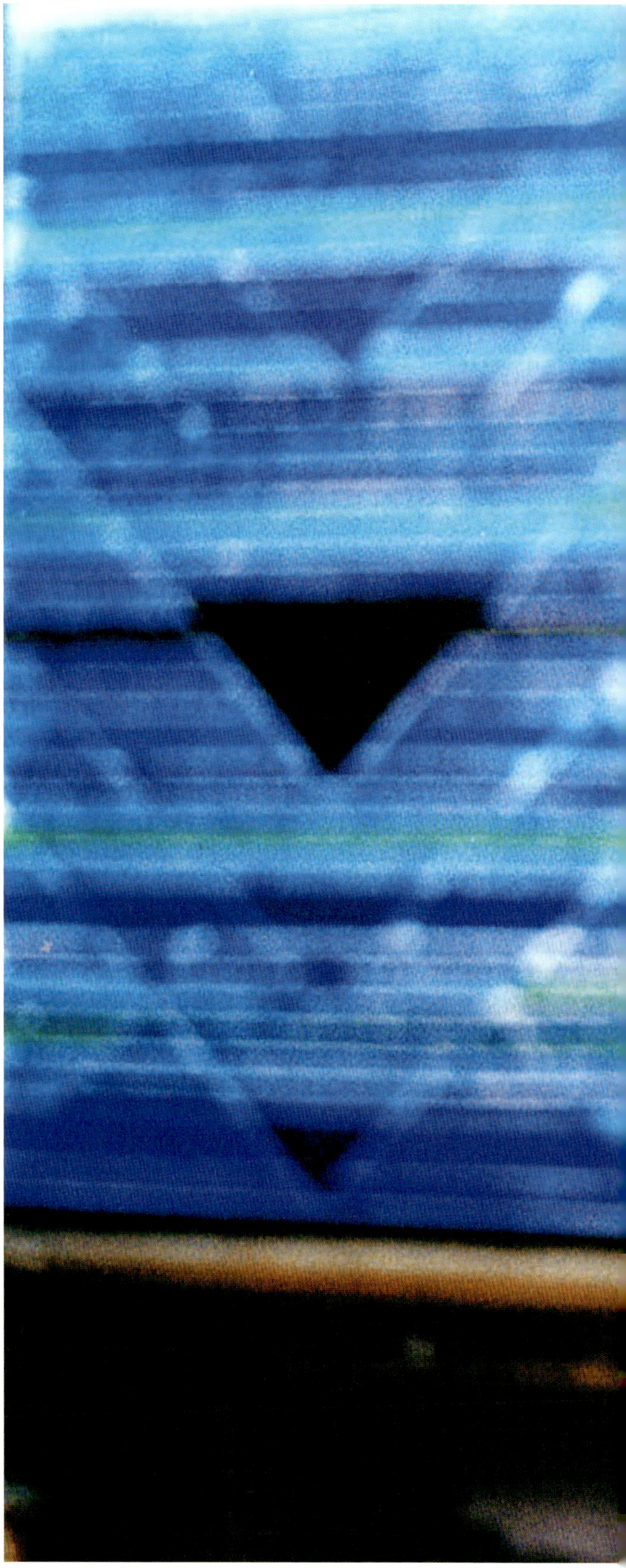

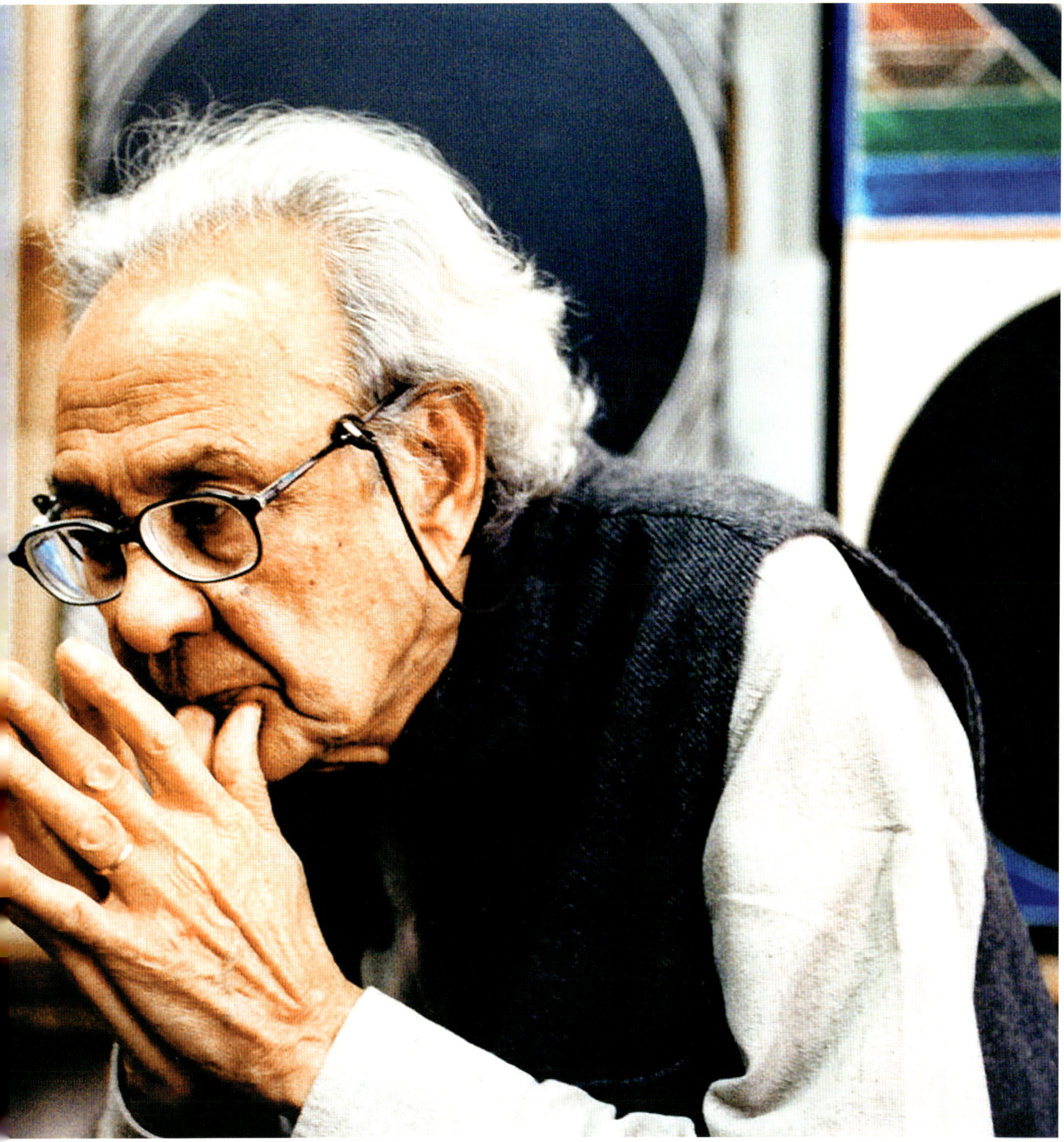

Raza did not observe any rituals but sought through different religions true and enduring spiritual communion. Here again I feel that the unique spiritual institution the Mahatma created in the 'Prarthana Sabha' with renditions of multi-religious scriptures and meditative silence was the inspiration behind Raza's practice.

—Ashok Vajpeyi

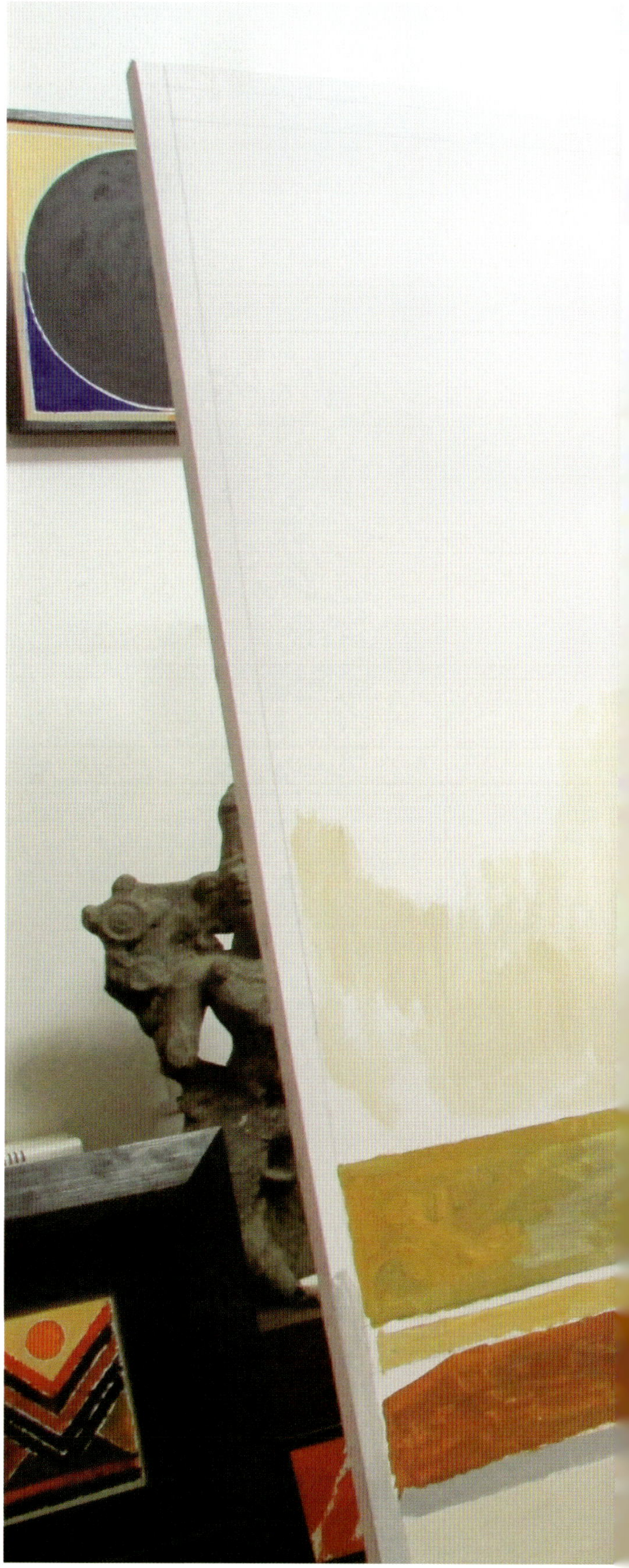

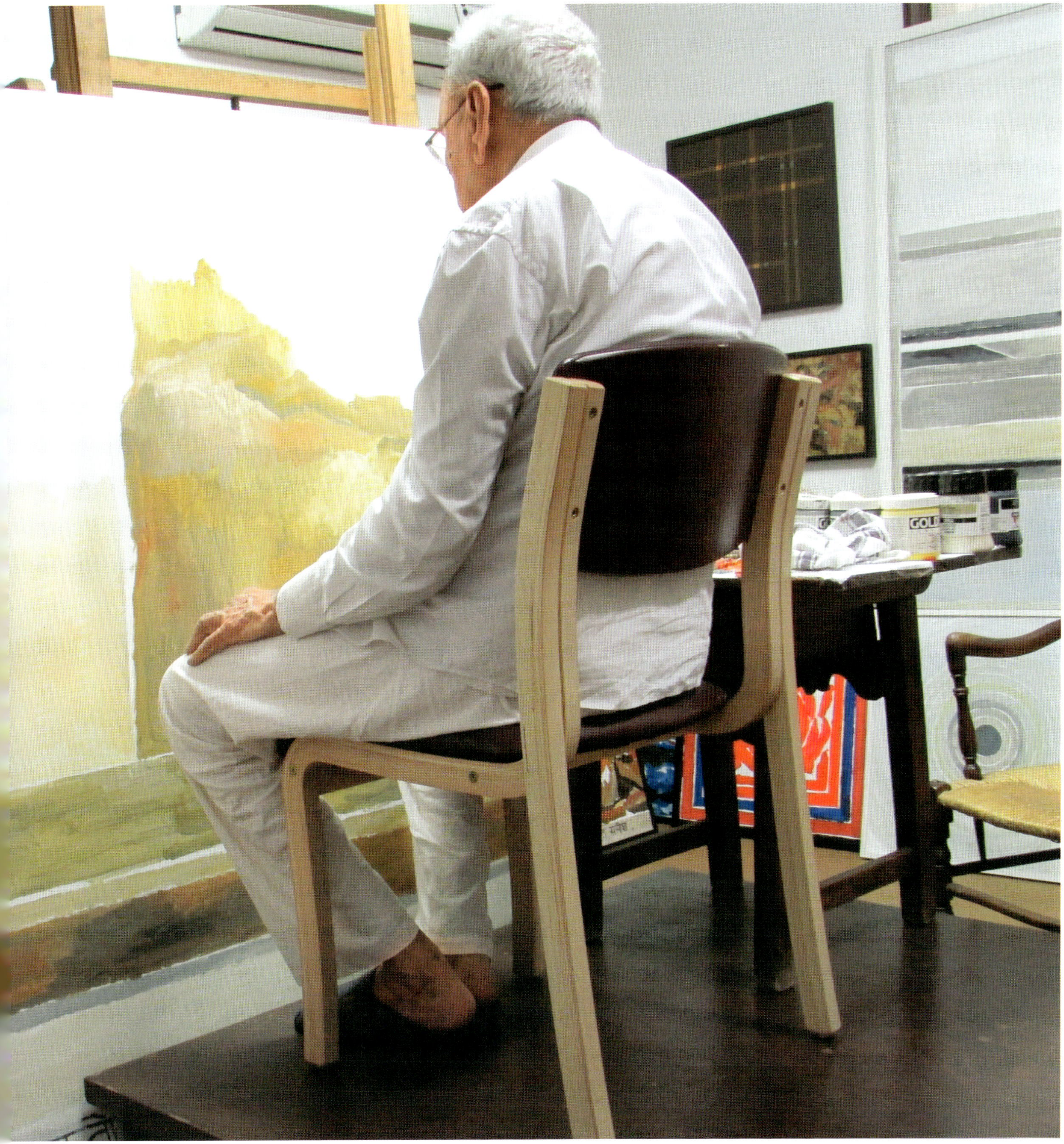

The Moral Aesthete in Gandhi GOPALKRISHNA GANDHI

Pearl S. Buck wrote a brief and incisive assessment of Gandhi on his 75th birthday[1]. The novelist said: "All great men have been reproached and derided and sometimes laughed at. It is Gandhi's greatness that he has ignored the derision and accepted the laughter and has continued to be himself. Somehow that self still stands intact, and laughter is dying down and derision is becoming quite futile".

A person who holds his or her self intact is a person of integrity. There is a wholeness to that person, an inner cohesion, a collectedness. An integer of thought or experience holds that person together. Whether that indivisibility is or is not a moral attribute, it certainly has an aesthetic dimension to it. Any artistic expression has to hold, hold together. A person with an inner resolve and a propulsion that takes it forward must express that resolve through words or actions that stand intact. Holding oneself intact means having a clear selfness, being brave enough to express that selfness, unafraid of the smite of derision, the laceration of cynical laughter or the loneliness of inattention. It also means being indifferent to acclaim.

The festschrift that published Pearl Buck's essay also carried Albert Einstein's better known, oft-quoted tribute to Gandhi: "Generations to come will scarce believe...." That deservedly celebrated tribute also contained the following lesser-known, rarely-quoted description of Gandhi: "A man who has confronted the brutality of Europe with the dignity of the simple human being and thus at all times risen superior." Neither the novelist nor the theoretical physicist had met Gandhi and yet both captured his essentiality, holding intact the simple dignity of a human being.

But Gandhi held his selfness intact for reasons other than the inner compactness of his 'self'. He did so in order to use it for purposes beyond his own inner satisfaction or personal fulfilment.

Artists impelled by a vision, a thought or an experience need to embrace it, hug it close. They need to own it and be owned by it in a relationship that is personal—so personal that it is beyond intimacy. And yet at the same time, they have to and need to give expression to it. To not express the vision or experience, to not reveal and share it, is to turn a mine into a hoard, a treasure into a closet. It is aesthetically vulnerable.

Every human being, often unbeknownst to oneself, has an unfledged epistemology. There is in every single one of them—in us—an uncut key to the riddle of life, a sound that is yet to become a word, a brush yet to taste paint, a note yet to discover its site in the seven *svaras* or somewhere, anywhere, in the ocean that heaves between them. And very individualistically, in an internally-held patent, is every person's very personal and very unique sense of beauty, of order, and an opposite of these two. This sense, actuated by the five senses but monitored by an unfathomable sixth, is describable as a person's 'A.Q.'—Aesthetic Quotient.

In its integrated vocabulary, its coordinated syntax, its seamless idiom and in its entirety, Gandhi's A.Q. rested on what he called 'truth' and 'non-violence'. And both were synchronous with his perception of beauty. Not Truth and Beauty, with the first letters in upper case, but his truth and his beauty. This A.Q. of his, immediately and inescapably brings to mind Keats's "beauty is truth, truth beauty—that is all / Ye

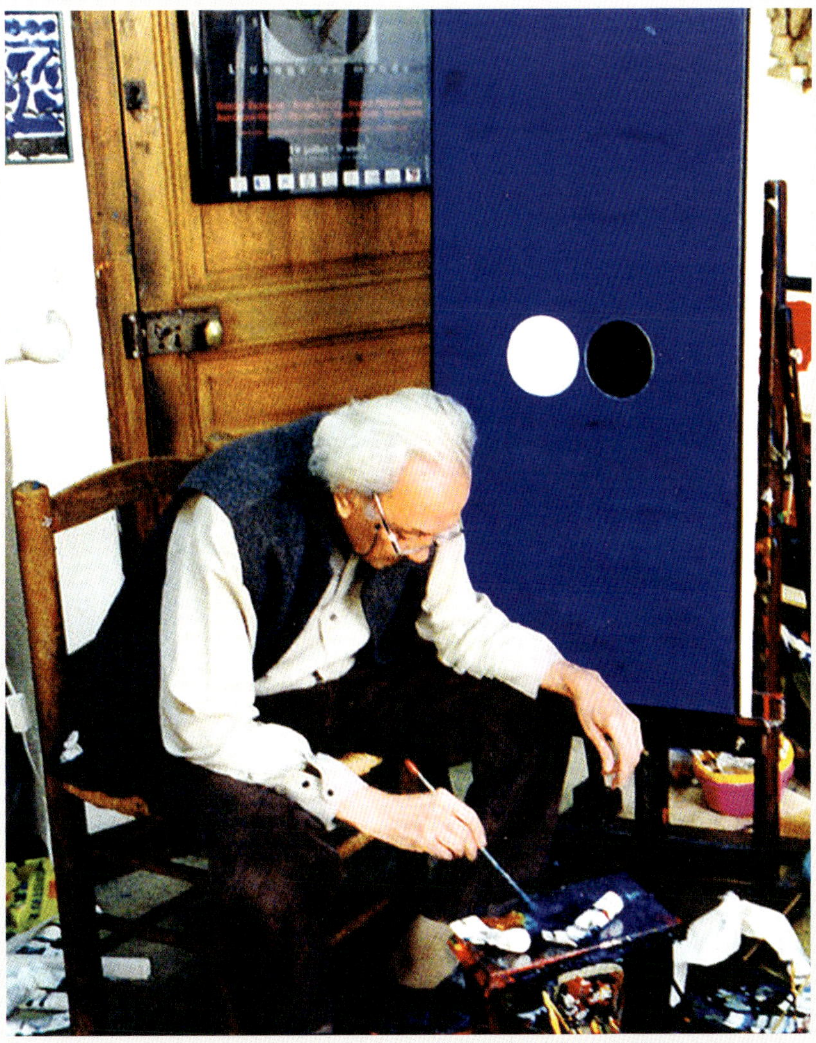

know on earth, and all ye need to know". To amalgamate what Pearl Buck and Einstein have said about him, his A.Q. held intact and it told him that violence grossly violated, simple human dignity. The 'modern way of life' which in its politico-economic aspect incorporated colonialism, imperialism, industrialism and, in a stunningly futuristic vision, modern consumerism and also environmental degradation, was in Gandhi's mind a brutal way of life. What is brutal is valuationally corrupt and aesthetically gross. That 'way' was, to him, erroneous, flawed and dangerous. Conversely, the way that is not violent, not brutal, not exploitative, was in his scheme the right way, the true way. He never described truth as beauty or beauty as truth but he stood, body, mind and heart held intact, in that intersection.

The English noun 'compassion' is used with some condescension today. It suggests benignity. And yet in its original sense conveyed by the Sanskrit *karuna*, the Tamil *parivu* or the Urdu *hamdardi* it is about the heart's response to another's suffering. And that response comes from one's activated conscience and one's actuated A.Q.

Ethics and aesthetics fluxed early for Gandhi. He writes[2] about his childhood days (Gujarati words used by him in the original are given in brackets): "There came to our place around that time itinerant showmen. Shravana carrying, by means of slings fitted from his shoulders, his blind parents on a pilgrimage was one of the pictures painted on glass I was shown. The book and the picture left an indelible impression on my mind. The agonising lament *(vilap)* of the parents over Shravana's death is still fresh in my memory. The tender verse *(lalitchhand)* moved me deeply and I played it on a music box *(vajun)* which my father had procured for me. I liked learning to play musical instruments."[3]

Gandhi's description of what must have been a local variant of Chinese lanterns and his sincere confession that he liked to play musical instruments show an early articulation of his A.Q. What, to me, makes the passage just quoted remarkable is his description of the verse sung as *lalitchhand*, a beautiful phrase to describe an experience that was at once moral and musical.

To close upon his sense of the heart-movingly beautiful, was his apprehension of the mind-disturbingly ugly. He writes: "I have seen in my childhood in Porbandar cows freely eating human faeces. This appeared to me revolting and the feeling has persisted to this day." A Manichean divide between what is true and beautiful on the one hand and what is true and revolting grew early in him as did the strengthening of an instinct to oppose and resist what jarred on him.

The sense of right and wrong and the agnatically related sense of what children are taught to distinguish as 'good' and 'bad', grows into a part-instinctive and part-learnt sense of 'lovely' and 'ugly'. His mother's conditioning of his adolescent mind certainly was at work when he reacted, as a student in London, to the sight of drunkenness with: "...those great palaces called public houses in London, where people went in as sober men and came out...dead drunk".[4] Foods have their own cultural aesthetics and the young Gandhi's Gujarati palate pampered by the centuries' old culinary subtleties of Kathiawar was completely dissatisfied with what London had to offer him. He told a gathering at London's Waverly Restaurant, "Oil and butter play an important part in the preparation of vegetables (back home)...I never saw a boiled potato in India".[5] But he was soon to develop not just a tolerance but also a taste for un-spiced foods.

One may cavil at Gandhi's turning his instincts and taught-behaviour into acute angles of moral evaluation, but then everyone's A.Q. grows out of unusual and individual stimuli. Visiting the Great Paris Exhibition in 1890, he went to see "the particular attraction of the Exhibition" namely, the Eiffel Tower. The 1000-feet high curiosity made wholly of iron got this description from the young law student: "There is no art about the Eiffel Tower...It was the toy of the Exhibition. We are all children attracted by trinkets".[6]

A preference for the small and the simple, the modest and the unostentatious seems to have taken him over even when he was a student and then a lawyer in South Africa. He used the term 'Negro' when describing the typical Zulu physique, the Zulu way of life and the Zulu hut. That word—Negro—offends the reading eye today. It offends the history, the politics, the civilization readers but, most importantly, the aesthetic reader. One wishes Gandhi's A.Q. had substituted the then standard description by another, like 'African'. But there it is, 'Negro', compromising one's appreciation of Gandhi's extraordinary celebration of the Zulu. Describing the Zulu hut in terms an architect would acknowledge as being accurate, he says: "They have a single round wall and are thatched with hay. A pillar inside supports the roof... It is said the Negroes cannot make anything square in shape. They have trained their eyes to see and (their hands to) make only round things. We never find nature drawing straight lines or rectilinear figures...."[7]

'Art and craft' were inextricably inter-woven in Gandhi's sensibility, the latter in fact driving the former. In learning to make and then going on to design what were, essentially, utilitarian devices, he derived as great an aesthetic pleasure as anyone would from painting, sculpting or writing 'for writing's sake'. His signet or 'stamp' in all these creations was minimalism. The austere, the stark, the immediately self-explicatory, was what worked with and for him. This also meant a low if not zero waste of material, even of lines in design. Flourishes were a luxury, an indulgence which neither time nor resources, permitted. Ingenuity lay in achieving the greatest impact, in beauty and utility, with the least deployment of resources—tangible and intangible. Just as his writing was strictly to the purpose, not an extra word weighing down the intent, so was what he created with his hands.

Conservation for him was another form of creation. Repairing, darning, re-cycling, the ability to renew, testified 'artisanship'. What is the difference between an artist and an artisan? His answer may well have been: 'To my mind, none'. Art, craft and cleanliness, likewise, were a threesome. Hygiene for him was necessary for human well-being, not as a medical norm but as a life-form. Asepsis was about medical and aesthetic intelligence. Suspending on a rope from the ceiling a tiltable garden watering can be a perfect bath shower—something he gave to his family and colleagues in South Africa.

Shoes and socks being used through mindless habit in hot climes was, for him, a horror. He learnt from his architect friend Hermann Kallenbach (who had observed the craft classes of a Trappist Monastery in Mariannhill, west of Durban) the fine art of making leather sandals. He used a basic three-strap design that gripped the forefoot, midfoot and hindfoot firmly, leaving the heel and toes free to breathe. Along with his colleagues, Gandhi made dozens of such pairs for kith, kin and for an unlikely user—his principal adversary in South Africa, the then Minister for the Interior, General Jan Smuts. Gifting Smuts that pair to mark the relatively satisfactory conclusion of their tormented engagement on the 'Indian Question', Gandhi literally added to the craft of diplomacy.

To resist the coagulated wrongs that he saw in South Africa he brought into effect, after written consultations with Leo Tolstoy and after reading Ruskin and Thoreau, the idea and action of passive resistance which in the variant he developed, he called "satyagraha". 'Soul force' is how *satyagraha* has been described. A telling description of what *satyagraha* means (rather than a translation of the word itself) is 'steadfast unto the truth'. That steadfastness was of course intended to be a supremely political move. But it was also an intrinsically aesthetic position. Anyone's truth, feeling, realisation has to be held, held on to, steadfastly. 'Sur pakad, sur pakad' (hold the note, hold the note) is an instruction which an exacting teacher of Hindustani music gives to the eager student, or 'srutisettupaadu, srutisettupaadu' in the Carnatic tradition. Holding the note intact in music, the brush sure on the canvas, the chisel sharp on the stone, the adze on leather, is both an aesthetic impulsion and a creative resolve.

As the master spinner of cotton yarn, Gandhi, later in India, fine-tuned the *charkha* to make it mobile, light, more serviceable than its archetypes. He also popularized the hand-held *takli* or 'drop spindle'. The trick of using which, also applicable to classical singing, was all about holding of the spindle at a particular angle, letting the yarn grow out of the sliver at a particular thickness, so that it can wind itself in a cone that does not go beyond the diameter of the metal disc. 'Sur pakad' (hold the note) and 'sutpakad' (hold the yarn) are both about staying intact. And that, did not just make a substitute for Lancashire cottons but also what Jawaharlal Nehru came to describe as 'the livery of freedom'.

Khadi and village industries were meant by him to be liberating devices, generating self-respect, self-reliance and dignity in what Einstein described as the "simple human being", as opposed to the brutality of

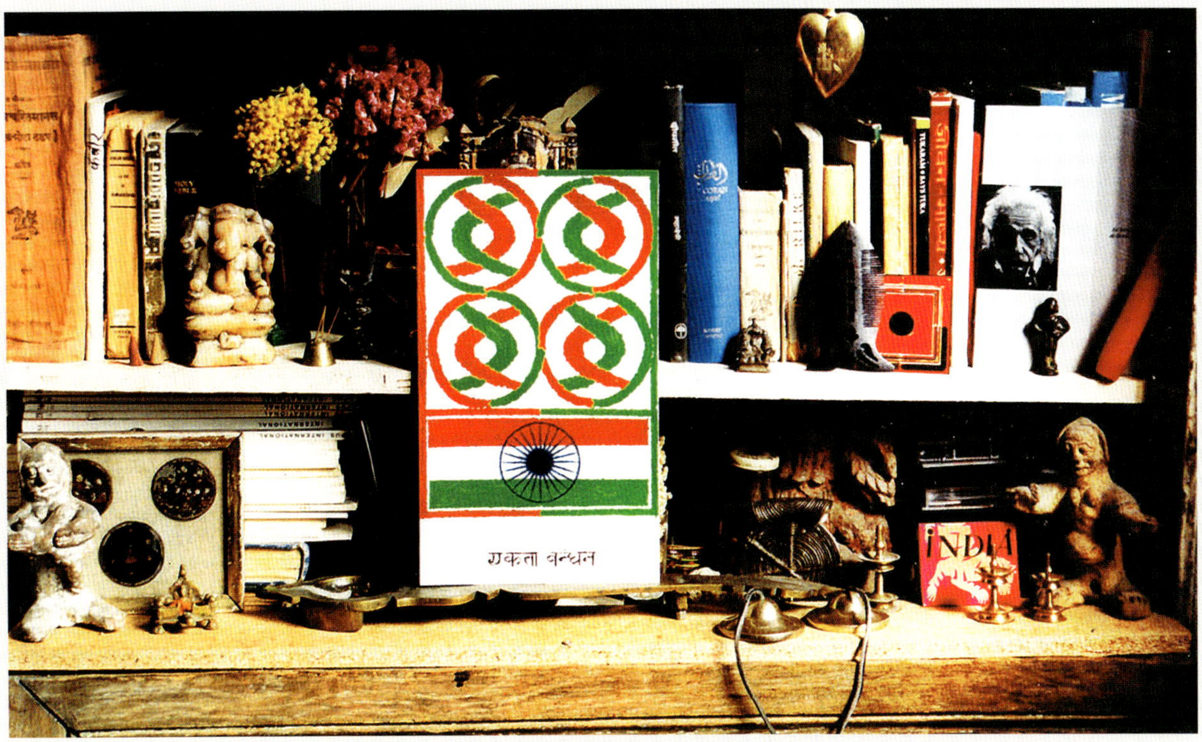
एकता बन्धन
INDIA

industrial behemoths. As Venu Madhav Govindu and Deepak Malghan have pointed out, Gandhi's intention, so passionately advocated by the economist J C Kumarappa, was to create a new line, a new path for India away from "the trajectory of commodification and mass production...on cultural and aesthetic grounds".[8]

After a visit to Chettinad in 1927, he wrote[9] to his Nattukkottai Chettiar hosts that their houses were "choked with foreign fineries and foreign things". His criticism was not just of the 'Europeanization' of things but was more intrinsic. "This lavish display", he wrote "obstructs the free flow of pure air and it harbours dust and so many million germs that float in the air". And then he went on to offer help by saying, "If you give me a contract for furnishing all these palaces of Chettinad I would furnish them with one-tenth of the money..." It is a matter of no small gratification that the offer was not accepted for a great many art objects and furniture of great beauty would then have been lost to antiquarian shops.

Great and gifted photographers apart, sculptors and painters sought out the counter-artist in Gandhi in his life-time. Mukul Dey did a stunning sketch of a very strong forty-nine years old Gandhi in Madras in 1918. Kanu Desai did a fifty-nine year old Mahatma in 1928, Nandalal Bose made the famous woodcut of the strident Mahatma on 12 April, 1930. J H Amshewitz painted him from life in 1931, Elizabeth Brunner did the same in Coonoor in 1934, Feliks Topolski did several sketches and one spectacular oil on canvas in the late 1940s.

All of them were seeking—and finding—in a somewhat reluctant and difficult subject an unusual aesthetic fascination. He drew them by the absence of clutter in him, his sparseness, the filament lightness of his physicality charged by an uncommon, almost unknown, moral voltage. Sayed Haider

Raza's Gandhi-inspired works of an unearthly, almost astral intangibility, suggest a strength that is beyond power, a stature that is independent of status. They hold secure that 'self' which Gandhi, in his thought, word and actions, held intact.

~

NOTES

1 *Gandhiji: His Life and Work*, eds. D.G. Tendulkar et al., Bombay: Karnataka Publishing House, October 2, 1945

2 From Gandhi's autobiography *The Story of Experiments with Truth* [translated from the original in Gujarati: *Satyana Prayogo athava Athmakatha* (Navajivan, 1927)]

3 *Collected Works of Mahatma Gandhi* (CWMG) Vol. 65, p. 100

4 CWMG, op. cit., Vol. 26, p. 390

5 CWMG, op. cit., Vol. 1, p. 40

6 Autobiography, op. cit., p. 47

7 *Satyagraha in South Africa* (Navajivan, 1928), pp. 8-9

8 *The Web of Freedom : J.C. Kumarappa and Gandhi's Struggle for Economic Justice* (Oxford University Press, 2016), p. 93

9 CWMG, op. cit., Vol. 35, pp. 19-20

I believe that all the great religions of the world are true more or less. I say 'more or less' because I believe that everything that the human hand touches, by reason of the very fact that human beings are imperfect, become imperfect.

~Mahatma Gandhi

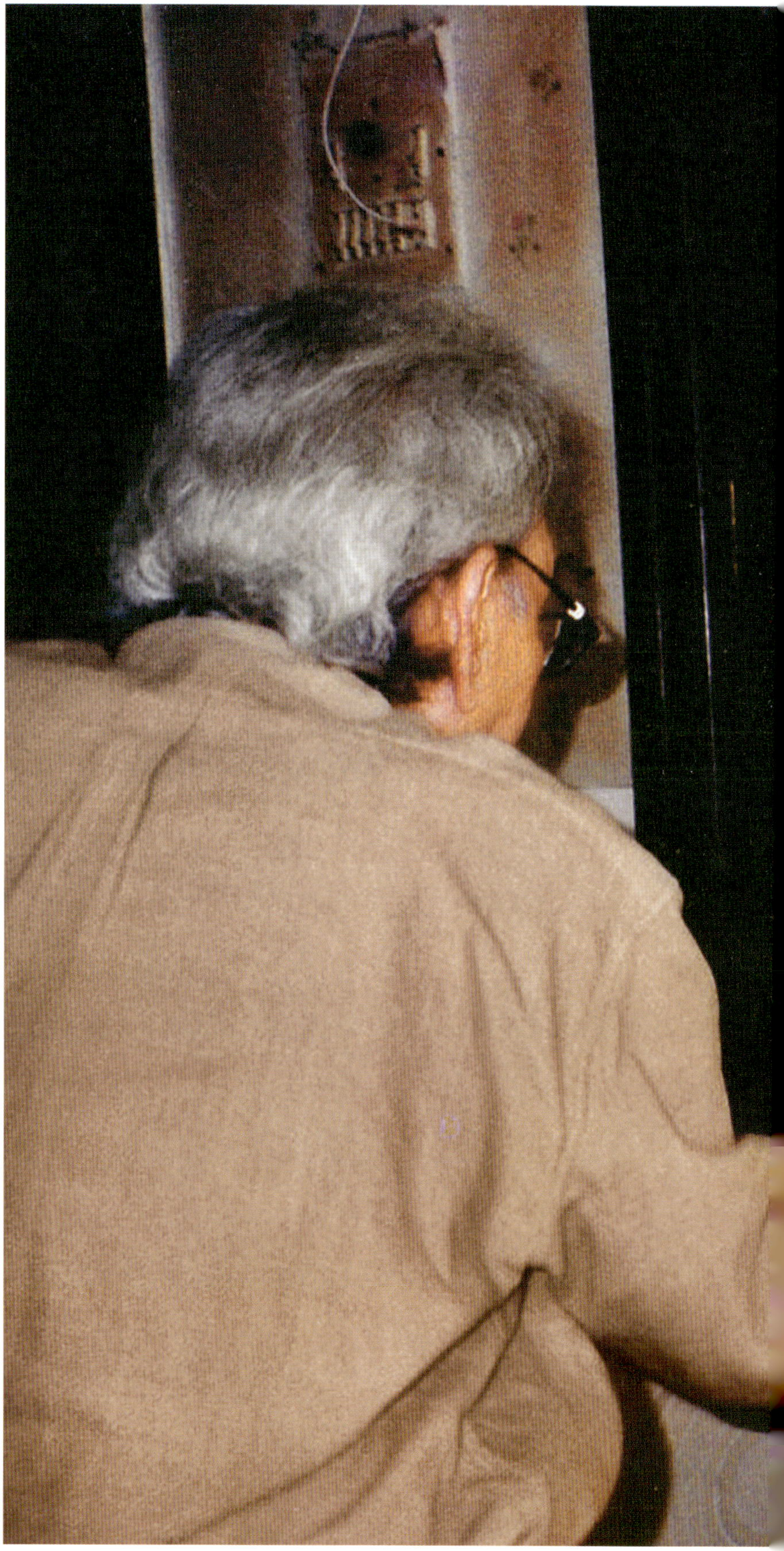

Painting 'Shanti' in Paris, 2000

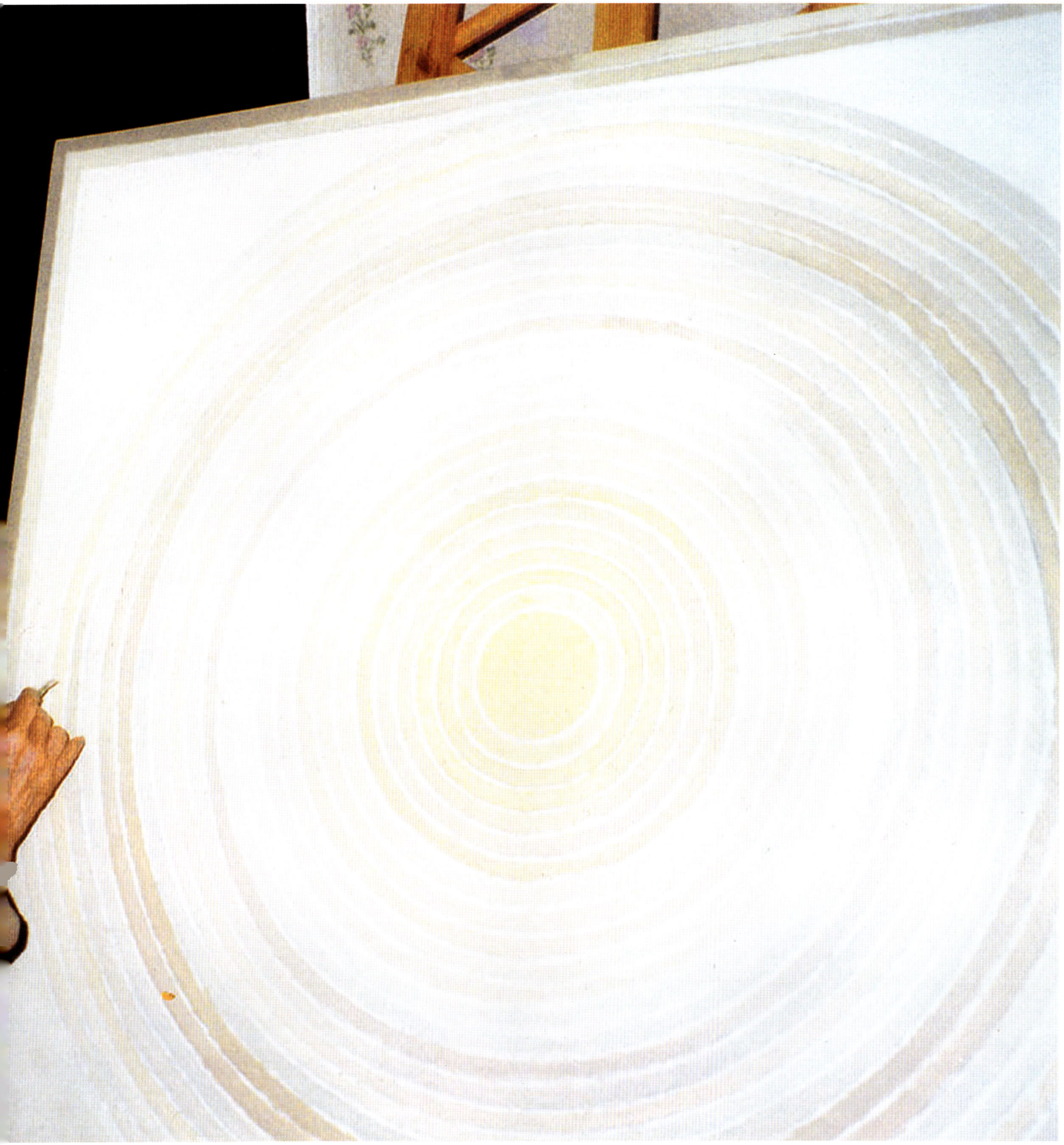

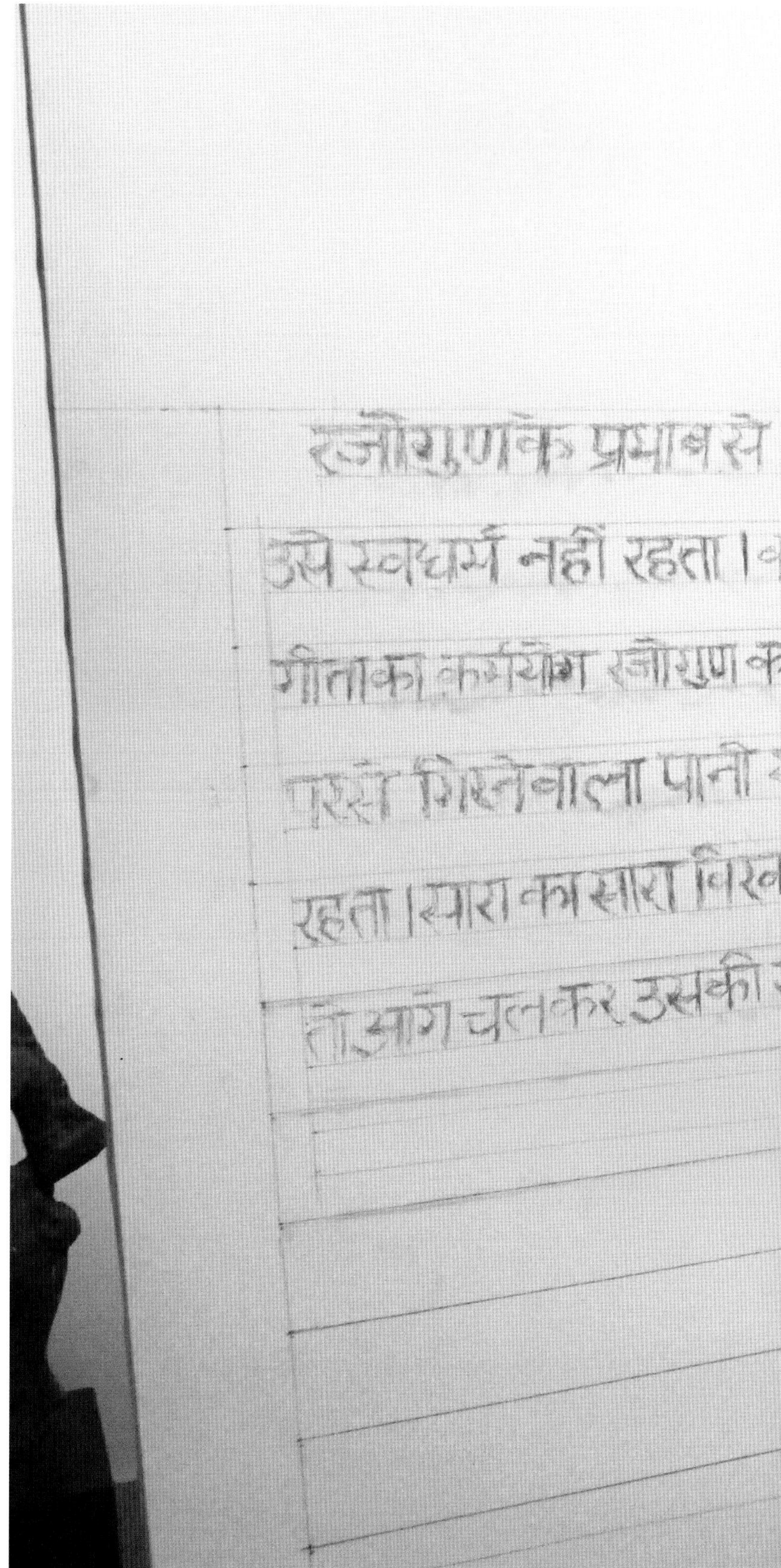

Raza in thought at his studio in New Delhi, 2013

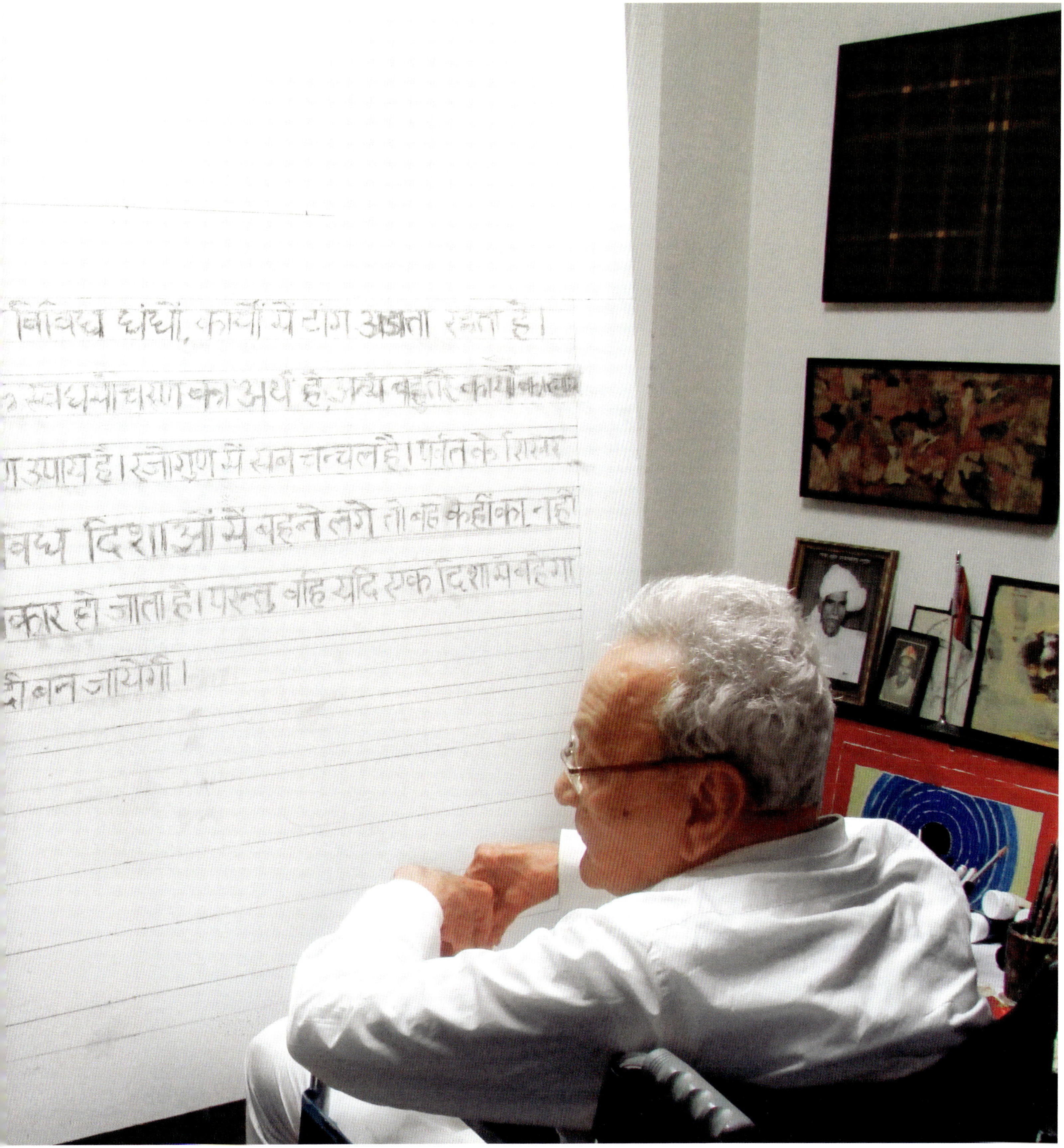

Bapuji[1] NANDALAL BOSE

Mridula ben[2] has asked me to write something on Bapuji. This has put me into some embarrassment. Language, after all, is not my medium. Moreover, to air my feelings for so intimately dear a person is both awkward and uncomfortable. I know the plea is useless. But wasn't this why I called him 'Bapu', and not 'Mahatmaji'? We have deep love for each other; a bond of affinity has been forged between us that's all. And this disinterested love shall endure. It is endless.

He is strong and pure, noble and fearless in his concern for doing good to others. He has love for all men, limitless compassion for all creatures, and he has staked his life for restoring a degenerate and oppressed land to its former glory. For even his ignorant adversary he has only pity and non violence. His indomitable power and defiance of death derive chiefly from his self-possession and complete lack of self-interest.

Anguish for human misery has turned him into an unpossessing hermit working for the well-being of others all the time. He has subdued his senses, and has accepted God as his chosen. These attributes of Mohandas Karamchand Gandhi overwhelm me.

What a miracle took place when, yearning for India's freedom, Gandhiji went on the Dandi march![3] The entire country was roused with confidence in some unique strength. Glory filled my heart. I felt blessed and life became meaningful.

After that, when I came to learn that he also had deep trust and affec tion for Dwijendranath Tagore[4]—the revered thinker, and for Gurudeva—the prince of poets, and that he considered Santiniketan too as his own home, he became another ashramite for us.

Being a painter, I perceive more through the eyes than through the ears. So I looked for a chance to see him in the flesh. Around that time, I received a letter from him asking me to set up an exhibition of Indian paintings during the Congress session at Lucknow[5]. The authority behind that call was clear. Any show of reluctance was just not possible. I was deeply worried at being asked to take such responsibility in an unfamiliar environment but could not turn down his call. The task, however, was fulfilled with his blessings; I was gratified to meet Bapu personally and at being able to see those paintings as well. I had been told before that Bapu did not have much interest in fine arts. I realized the mistake when I found him going round the Lucknow Exhibition and noticing each painting with the critical interest of a connoisseur.

His sense of beauty and harmony was revealed to me by a small incident. With reeds, bamboos and timber the exhibition hall had been decorated in a simple manner. We carefully saw to it that aesthetic demands were not sacrificed. For the first time the general public had a chance to see how much beauty could be generated by using very ordinary things, though we ourselves were accustomed in the ashrama to decorate in this very simple fashion. Bapuji endorsed this kind of aesthetic creativity and so he fully enjoyed it and expressed pleasure at the work of the artists. The incident I want to point out is this: though everything was neatly arranged in the exhibition hall, someone had carelessly left a bucket under a table. It escaped our eyes but not the sharp eyes of Bapuji. On entering the hall he noticed it at once, and observed:

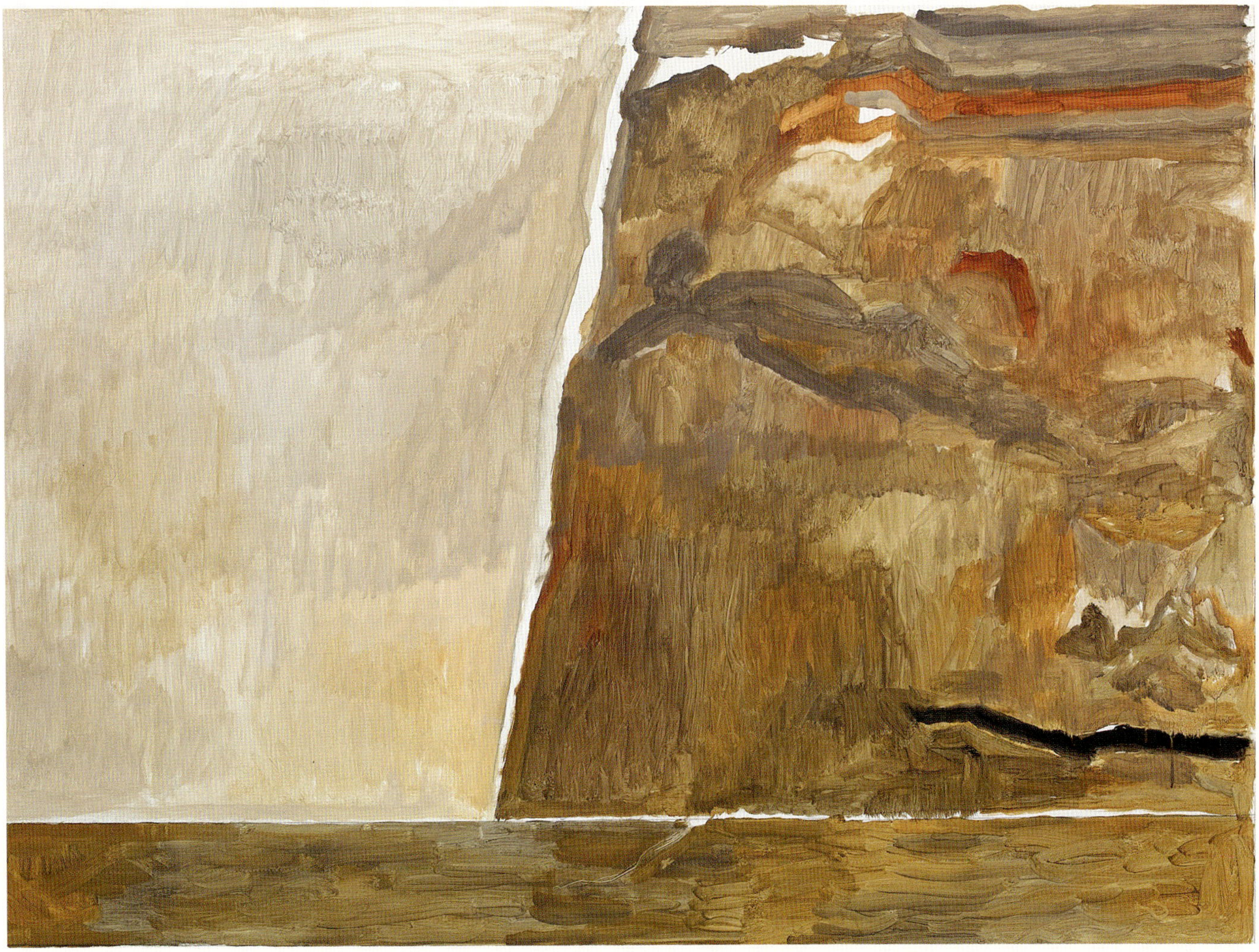

"Doesn't that disturb your sense of beauty?" He visited the hall everyday and spent there a lot of time. Later, before the Village Congress[6] session at Faizpur, he wrote me another letter: "You are being given the charge of decorating the entire Congress Nagar". The letter added: "A little does not satisfy, the heart demands more"—this must have been because he had liked the exhibition at the Lucknow Congress —"So come and see me at Sevagram". "But I am a painter, and know nothing about architecture, I am not, therefore, the right man for the task", I pleaded in my reply. He wrote back a beautiful letter and thereby enlisted my services. The main point of the letter was: "I need no expert pianist. I want a warm-hearted fiddler".

So I went to Sevagram. Mahadev Desai[7] led me to his presence. In the cottage at Sevagram, face to face with that great man, I squatted on the floor. "Come closer", he insisted. Knees touched knees. I took the dust of his feet. He did not object, rather willingly accepted it. His pity melted my heart into heavenly love. His eyes were clear, as if probing the depths of one's heart. I felt an urge to lay open my heart for his inspection and to tell him all I wanted to tell. His heavenly smile could melt the heart even of a confirmed villain. Forceful words, no faltering, no obscurity, like chips of a diamond. And I noted that he started answering even before I had completed asking a question as if his heart fathomed my heart. Words were unimportant.

He commanded, "Go to Faizpur", even before I had a chance to begin. He was at that time nursing Meerabai[8]. An American clergy-man was shown in who wanted to ask him about his notion of the appropriate form of future religion in India, as well as about his personal faith. Bapu said he knew nothing about the form that religion would take in future and added, "as for the present, my religion is to serve others, as you are witnessing now". Then he turned to Mahadev and said, "Ask Jamnalal[9] to send someone with him. He shall show him around Faizpur[10], and then put him on the train for Bolpur."

He gave me three letters, one for the secretary at Faizpur, one for Ramdasji Gulati, the engineer, and the third for Vinobaji[11] with this instruction to me: "I am sure you would be happy to meet Vinobaji, a warm-hearted holy man. He gave up everything for the good of the country. You must especially see him." I visited Faizpur, inspected the venue; and also met Vinobaji. Then I discussed with Ramdasji and chalked out the plan. When I came back Bapu's only instructions were, "Build the township at Faizpur using only rural material and employing country craftsmen. The conception should be indigenous. As for the decoration part you are in sole charge. Ramdasji and other members would give you any kind of assistance you need." What trust! He was completely at ease putting all the responsibility on my shoulders. Keeping him in mind, I also gradually gathered necessary strength for the novel assignment.

A few months later I went back with four of my students (Perumal[12], Kanai[13], Mehta[14], and Prabhat[15]), and spent a few months working on the assignment. Somehow everything was completed to our satisfaction. Assistance came from unexpected quarters. Engineer Ramdasji and Vinobaji's disciple Methy Master gave us a lot of support and ever since both have been my dear friends.

It was at Faizpur that I noticed for the first time what a profound regard the rural people cherished for Bapuji. He first conceived the Gram Congress at Faizpur, and it proved to be a resounding success though many people had initially dismissed the idea as absurd. He offered unstinted praise for the artists, and was greatly pleased with the main entrance gate made of bamboos. Jawaharlalji came as the President of the session. Decorated with ornamental hangings made in the village, a chariot was put together with bamboos draped with cloth. It was drawn by six pairs of bullocks to bring him to the conference site. Bapu called for me one day and said, "I have made a bet with a girl, who is like my grand-daughter, on your ability to make a duplicate chariot of the kind that you have made to carry Jawaharlal, only the bullocks this time would be mock-bullocks. It would be kept in the exhibition ground. I give you two days to do it." And then added, "see that I can win the bet." Our artist-group was highly amused at that challenge. My students and I set to work, and six pairs of bullocks were created with slit bamboos and painted. They were hitched up to a chariot and placed at the exhibition ground. Bapuji won the bet. Looking at those mock-bullocks and the chariot he burst into laughter that I can never forget. He was just like a child, immensely pleased with winning a bet. I realized at once how much he enjoyed a work of art. During his address at the conference, too, he dwelt extensively on art, and paid homage to the artistic glory of India.

Another call came at the time of the Haripura Congress[16]. On that occasion also I spent some months decorating the conference grounds. A large number of students also worked with me. This time the instruction was to make the exhibition clearly visible to the rural people passing by. "Cover the entire area", he suggested, "with examples of art". Following the *pat* style we did a large number of paintings and hung them everywhere—on the main entrance, inside volunteers' camps, even in the rooms meant for Bapuji and Subhasbabu[17], the President. These occasions convinced me that he deeply appreciated fine arts and

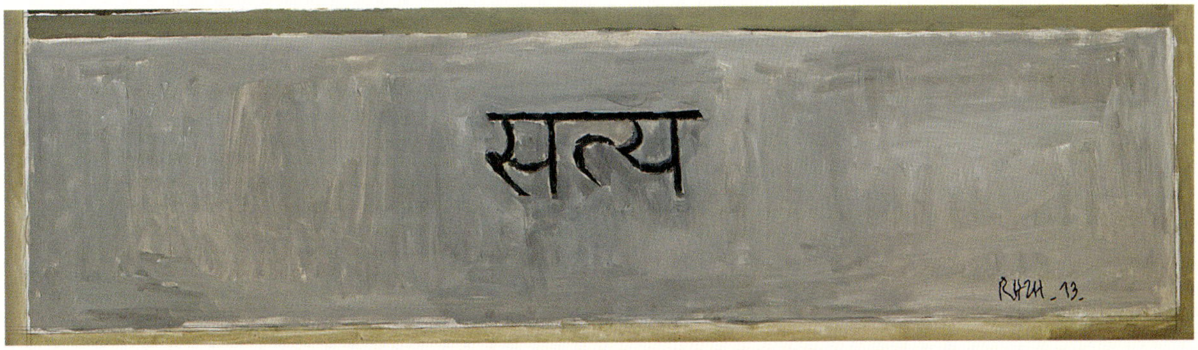
सत्य

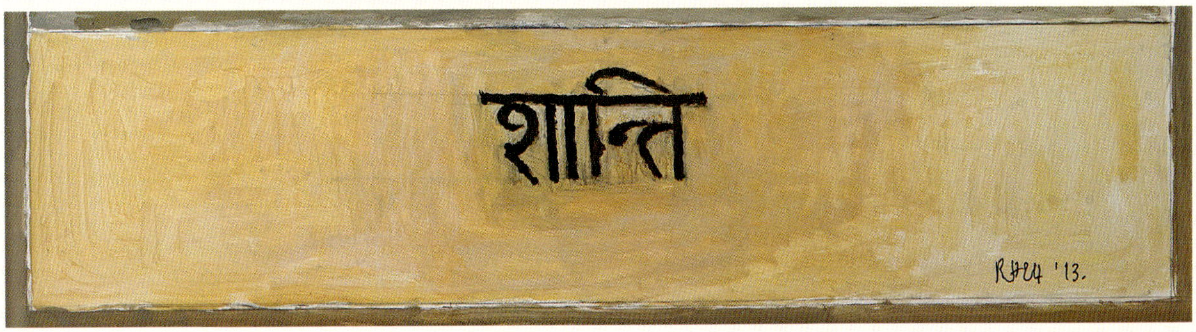
शान्ति

was its champion. Or else why did he express so much delight in seeing these? We also organized there an exhibition of paintings. The day Bapu came to visit it I know why he first smiled at me and asked, "Still alive?" Almost everyone at Haripura was down with malaria; everyone was ill while I had been spared. I replied, "I am rather in better health here." Those two words from Bapu stood for his appreciation and affection for me.

At the time of opening the khadi exhibition we decided on the ceremonial lighting of five lamps on a stand in place of cutting a tape at the door with a pair of scissors according to the foreign custom. He was pleased at this and delightedly told others how much more beautiful and meaningful this Indian custom was than the alien one. Evidently he loved the arts, particularly the glorious arts of his motherland.

Another time at Sevagram we were exchanging notes on art. I was there, invited by Jamnalalji for the restoration of a temple and for doing some fresco work. The condition of the temple did not permit any restoration. During our conversation he raised the question of building a new temple altogether. Imbued with modern ideas we objected, and said, "why should we have more temples?" At this he remained silent for a long time, and then said, "Temples have got to be built time and again. Because mankind, ever on the move, would continue to realize new forms of truth, and these have to be enshrined for adoration. How can the temples of eternal truth ever be allowed to disappear?"

He told us another thing on that occasion. Since I still had some misgivings that he probably valued political matters more than fine art, I boldly raised the question one day. He confessed that fine art, particularly music, was very close to his heart. Music was so dear to him indeed that he would have completely devoted himself to that art hadn't he got involved in the country's struggle for freedom. Now there was no choice left for him. Commitments had been made and there was no going back for a life time. All the same, he concluded, he never ignored fine art. That he did was sheer calumny.

From Bapuji's life-style artists may find inspiration and develop their own character. Bapuji is indeed an artist and his creativity finds expression in the building up of his own self, in his attempt to transform himself from a man into a divine being, as also guide others in that direction. It is common knowledge that through his contact a large number of people have reached divinity. His thoughts have definiteness and clarity, his heart is pure, and he is ready to boldly sacrifice his life for the love of others. Thus he has conquered death. To dismiss his ideal is very difficult because he first practices himself what he preaches to others. Here is a rare human being whose clear heart is open for all to look into. He has absolutely nothing to hide, like clear sunlight. His words reflect his mind.

Indian artists, if they want, may transform themselves by following the model of his character. Without having a strong character an artist produces work that lacks force or foundation.

Most people fail to understand why Bapuji does not favour machine-made things. Certainly not because he cannot stand machines. Being an artist myself, I can fully vouch for his attitude. Machine-made articles may of course be useful, may even be economically beneficial for men and the country, but they can never satisfy the aesthetic need. This is where Bapuji is a patron of artists. Aesthetic quality *(rasa)* does not quite flourish where the stamp of the individual craftsmanship and temperament is absent. Expression of form is not universal, only the realization behind it is. Or else God's creation would not have this diversity. Diversity is typical of creativity. This is the specialty of all artists—even the human artist.

Rasa is invariably the same. Only individual artists give diverse expressions to it, and therein lies our joy. Lacking this diversity machine-made things tire the mind. When the mind dries up it affects the society at large. Wealth and prosperity may swell, but the heart remains starved. Men no longer tend, then, to become divine but lean towards brutality.

This is why artists love to work with simple materials and tools so that more of one's heart may then be poured into work. These lines from an unsure hand may kindly be taken as an act of veneration for a noble man who himself, I am sure, would pardon its inadequacies and accept it as an offering from a humble devotee. I know, his affection for me comes from the depth of his heart.

~

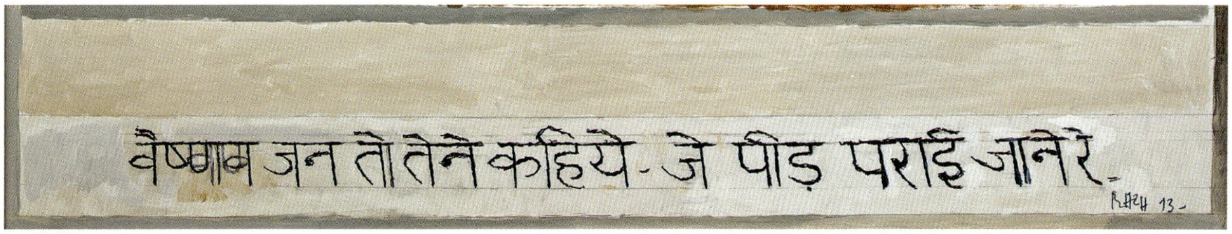

NOTES

1. Published in "The Visva-Bharati Quarterly" in December 1987
2. Mridula Sarabhai
3. April 1930
4. Eldest brother of Rabindranath Tagore
5. April 1936
6. December 1936
7. Gandhiji's private secretary
8. Mira ben – Mrs. Margaret Slade, Gandhiji's disciple
9. Jamnalal Bajaj
10. Congress session of 1936
11. Vinoba Bhave
12. Arunachala Perumal
13. Kanai Samanta
14. Jaipal Metha
15. Prabhatmohan Banerjee
16. February 1938
17. Subhas Chandra Bose

रज़ा फाउण्डेशन | THE RAZA FOUNDATION

THE RAZA FOUNDATION

Even when he was widely acknowledged as a major figure of modern Indian art, Sayed Haider Raza, living in France and Paris for sixty years, always felt deeply concerned about the struggles of and inadequate opportunities for the younger generations of artists in his native country. On his almost annual sojourns to India, Raza would always find time and the energy to meet young artists, see and discuss their works, and would invariably acquire the ones he felt had some substance of either idiom or vision. His mansion in Paris had a large and growing collection of such works.

Ever since he started earning sufficient income from his art, Raza deeply desired that at least a part of this income go towards the promotion and support of younger artists in India. Young Indian artists who visited him in Paris never tire of their tales of his unfailing generosity which eventually took the shape of the Raza Foundation, a private non-profit trust.

In the beginning the Foundation gave two awards annually, one in visual arts and one in poetry. Later the scheme expanded to cover classical music and classical dance also. Each award carried a sum of Rs. 1 lakh and a citation. It can be said without exaggeration that some of the best, the most innovative and daring artists, poets, musicians and dancers have been recipients of these highly coveted and prestigious awards; more so, because they were instituted by a great artist who has been the exclusive donor of his personal funds to the Foundation. Apart from the above-mentioned awards, the Raza Foundation, over the years, has also contributed towards publication of catalogues by young artists; intellectual and creative encounters; celebrations of birth centenaries of two major Hindi poets, Agyeya and Shamsher Bahadur Singh; and has been involved with art workshops in new media, international poetry festival with the Kritya Thiruvananthapuram, and other such events. Since 2009 the Foundation has been organizing a week-long interactive camp at Anandgram, New Delhi, featuring around 15 of the Raza Foundation awardees. The annual event allows practitioners of visual arts, music, dance and poetry to share ideas, visions, anxieties, etc., and to develop a deeper understanding of arts other than one's own.

Ashok Vajpeyi, initially the Life Trustee took over as the Managing Trustee in 2007 and Raza came back home, to India in 2011 to live in Delhi for good, after that the Foundation further expanded its activities under his unobtrusive and generous guidance. A new series of panel discussions on many urgent issues of the arts such as Democracy and Culture, Arts and Public Institutions, the Disappearing Criticism, etc., titled 'Art Matters' is already taking place in Delhi. 42 talks and conversations have taken place so far.

Seven memorial lectures named after some of the great masters namely V S Gaitonde (visual arts), Agyeya (poetry), Habib Tanvir (theatre), Kelucharan Mohapatra (dance), Kumar Gandharva (music), Mani Kaul (cinema), and Daya Krishna (philosophy) have also been held since 2012–13.

Also, apart from its usual awards, the Foundation also offered Raza fellowships to young scholars, critics, etc., in the fields of visual arts, poetry, music and dance. The Foundation supported two international seminars: 'Art and the Promise of Beauty' in February 2012 and 'Word and Image' in 2013. A Hindi journal of literature, arts and ideas, *Samas*, is being published by Raza Foundation and edited by Udayan Vajpeyi.

The Foundation has also been providing financial assistance for a large number of institutions, individuals and projects relating to culture, visual arts, music, dance, theatre, ideas, architecture, photography etc. They include a retrospective of Mani Kaul's films in Osian Film Festival, centenaries of Ram Vilas Sharma, Nalin Vilochan Sharma; 'Samanvya': a multilingual festival of letters, 'Sahmat', Khoj Studios, Kabir Project Bengaluru, centenary of Mohanrao Kalyanpurkar, 'Arts as Activism Exhibition', the Critical Collective website, 'Kaljayee': a festival celebrating 90th year of Kumar Gandharva etc.

The Foundation provided financial assistance for publication of many important books including *Art Critic: Writings of Richard Bartholomew*, *Kumar Shahani: The Shock of Desire and other essays*, *Smriti Vismriti: Shankho Chaudhury*, *Kaljayee Kumar Gandharva*, *The Spirit of Indian Paintings : B N Goswamy*, *Finding My Way: Venkat Singh Shyam*, *Sonata of Solitude : Vasudev Santu Gaitonde* etc.

āKāR pRaKāR

AKAR PRAKAR

Established in 2004 by Reena and Abhijit Lath, Akar Prakar is one of the leading galleries and promoters of Indian art today. Selected by Blouinart info as amongst the top 500 galleries worldwide, since 2012, Akar Prakar has a national presence with an international footprint. Akar Prakar works with various government agencies such as the NGMA, Ministry of Culture, Lalit Kala Akademi, ICCR and Indian and International museums in promoting Indian modern and contemporary art. It has also produced books and publications on some of the major artists in collaboration with the LKA and ICCR, NGMA, Ministry of Culture, and various private organizations.

With its continuing vision to showcase significant contemporary Indian art in distinguished museums and venues across the world, last year Akar Prakar executed 4 projects in France, along with the ICCR and the embassy of India in France, under Namaste France 2016. These projects were Jayashree Chakravarty's "Life Would Never Be the Same", with the KNMA (Kiran Nadar Museum of Art, New Delhi) at the Asiatique Museum in Nice, France; "Manish Pushkale, Painter of Light" at the Musee de Guethary; a show of master artist S H Raza and Manish Pushkale at Baudoin Lebon, Paris, and Debanjan Roy with a residency and show at Chateau de la Napoule, France. This year, besides art showings in India of Ganesh Pyne's rare early works, and Ganesh Haloi's solo of recent work; Akar Prakar will present Jayashree Chakravarty showcasing her artworks at the Musée Guimet in Paris, in collaboration with the KNMA, and Ganesh Haloi will be showcased in Athens and Kassel. These projects present a wide view of the contemporary art practices in India, along with opening dialogues between countries through the language of art.

This year, Akar Prakar is launching four major books on Indian art and artists. It has produced books on artists like Meera Mukherjee, Ganesh Pyne, in collaboration with the LKA; on Ganesh Haloi, and Jayashree Chakravarty, and also a volume on Indian crafts, its contemporary status with possible solutions, with Jaya Jaitley, as the guest editor for *artVarta*, Akar Prakar's biannual magazine on arts.

Reena and Abhijit Lath

Akar Prakar

CONTRIBUTORS

Nandalal Bose (1882–1966) was one of the pioneers of modern Indian art and a key figure of Contextual Modernism. A pupil of Abanindranath Tagore, Nandalal Bose was known for his 'Indian style' of painting. He became the principal of Kala Bhavan, Santiniketan in 1922. He was influenced by the Tagore family, E B Havell, A K Coomaraswamy and Mahatma Gandhi. Bose achieved fame not only for his renderings of plays by Rabindranath Tagore but also for his designing and execution of the venues of the Indian National Congress conventions in Lucknow, Faizpur and Haripura from 1935 to 1938. He was the only artist that Gandhi ever patronized. While he had already been internationally recognized as an important artist, his association with Gandhi elevated him to the status of national icon. In the year 1954, he was honored with the Padma Vibhushan award.

Gopalkrishna Gandhi (born 1946) is a former senior diplomat who has also served as Governor of West Bengal (2004–2009) and Secretary to the President of India K R Narayanan (1997–2002). As a former member of the Indian Administrative Service he served in Tamil Nadu and in Delhi, and also worked in India's diplomatic missions in South Africa, Lesotho, Sri Lanka, Norway and Iceland. To his name he has titles: *The Oxford Gandhi* (OUP, 2007), *A Frank Friendship: Gandhi and Bengal* (Seagull, 2008), *Of a Certain Age – Twenty Life-Sketches* (Penguin India, 2011), *My Dear Bapu: Correspondence between C Rajagopalachari and Mohandas Karamchand Gandhi, Devdas Gandhi and Gopalkrishna Gandhi* (Penguin, 2012), *The Tirukkural: A New English Version* (Aleph, 2015) and *The Death Penalty* (Aleph, 2016). A monthly columnist for *The Hindustan Times* (New Delhi), he also writes frequently for *The Hindu* (Chennai). Gopalkrishna Gandhi is currently the Professor of History and Politics at Ashoka University, Sonepat.

Ashok Vajpeyi (born 1941) is a Hindi poet, critic, editor, culture-activist and a close friend and aideof S H Raza. He is widely recognized for his contribution to the establishment of Bharat Bhavan in Bhopal, and has also served as the first Vice-Chancellor of the Mahatma Gandhi International Hindi University. In India, he has been awarded the Sahitya Akademi Award, the Dayawati Kavi Shekhar Samman and the Kabir Samman. After retiring as Chairman of the Lalit Kala Akademi, New Delhi in 2011 he is now Managing Trustee of the Raza Foundation and it is under his guidance that the Foundation has been hosting festivals of music, dance, literature, arts and theatre and also publishing books on various subjects relating to the arts. He has published over 23 books of poetry, criticism and art. He has also been honoured by the Governments of France and Poland.

Sayed Haider Raza (1922–2016) studied painting in India and after receiving a French Government scholarship in 1950 he left for the École Nationale des Beaux-Arts, Paris. Raza was awarded the Prix de la Critique in Paris in 1956. Though he worked and lived in France for 60 years, he maintained strong ties with India only to return to India in 2010. He established the Raza Foundation, New Delhi in 2001. The Government of India awarded him the Padma Shree, the Padma Bhushan and the Padma Vibhushan besides being conferred with the Légion d'Honneur by the French Government. His works are mainly abstracts replete with references and icons from Indian cosmology and its philosophy. His life and works reflect the influence of Mahatma Gandhi's ideas and vision.